Databa

CW00751055

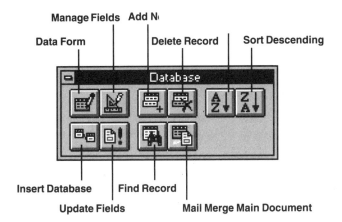

Manage Fields   Add N

Data Form

Delete Record   Sort Descending

Database

Insert Database   Find Record

Update Fields   Mail Merge Main Document

Header and Footer Toolbar

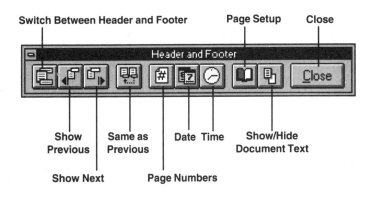

Switch Between Header and Footer   Page Setup   Close

Header and Footer

Close

Show
Previous

Same as
Previous

Date Time

Show/Hide
Document Text

Show Next   Page Numbers

The SYBEX Instant Reference Series

Instant References are available on these topics:

AutoCAD Release 12 for DOS

AutoCAD Release 12 for Windows

CorelDRAW 3

CorelDRAW 4

dBASE

dBASE IV 2.0 Programmer's

DOS 5

DOS 6

DR DOS 6

Excel 4 for Windows

Harvard Graphics 3

Harvard Graphics for Windows

Lotus 1-2-3 Release 2.3 & 2.4 for DOS

Lotus 1-2-3 Release 4 for Windows

Lotus 1-2-3 for Windows

Microsoft Access

Norton Desktop for DOS

Norton Desktop for Windows 2.0

Norton Utilities 7

OS/2 2.1

PageMaker 4.0 for the Macintosh

Paradox 4 Programmer's

Paradox 4 User's

Paradox for Windows User's

PC Tools 8

Quattro Pro for Windows

SQL

Windows 3.1

Windows NT

Word for Windows, Version 2.0

WordPerfect 5.1 for DOS

WordPerfect 5.1 for Windows

WordPerfect 6 for DOS

Computer users are not all alike.
Neither are SYBEX books.

We know our customers have a variety of needs. They've told us so. And because we've listened, we've developed several distinct types of books to meet the needs of each of our customers. What are you looking for in computer help?

If you're looking for the basics, try the **ABC's** series. For a more visual approach, select full-color **Quick & Easy** books.

Running Start books are two books in one: a fast-paced tutorial, followed by a command reference.

Mastering and **Understanding** titles offer you a step-by-step introduction, plus an in-depth examination of intermediate-level features, to use as you progress.

Our **Up & Running** series is designed for computer-literate consumers who want a no-nonsense overview of new programs. Just 20 basic lessons, and you're on your way.

SYBEX **Encyclopedias**, **Desktop References**, and **A to Z** books provide a comprehensive reference and explanation of all of the commands, features, and functions of the subject software.

Sometimes a subject requires a special treatment that our standard series don't provide. So you'll find we have titles like **Advanced Techniques, Handbooks, Tips & Tricks,** and others that are specifically tailored to satisfy a unique need.

You'll find SYBEX publishes a variety of books on every popular software package. Looking for computer help? Help Yourself to SYBEX.

For a complete catalog of our publications:

SYBEX Inc.
2021 Challenger Drive, Alameda, CA 94501
Tel: (510) 523-8233/(800) 227-2346 Telex: 336311
Fax: (510) 523-2373

Word 6 for Windows
Instant Reference

Sheila S. Dienes

SYBEX®

San Francisco • Paris • Düsseldorf • Soest

Developmental Editor: Sarah Wadsworth
Editor: Guy Hart-Davis
Technical Editor: Erik Ingenito
Production Artist: Suzanne Albertson
Screen Graphics: Cuong Le
Page Layout and Typesetting: Len Gilbert
Proofreader/Production Assistant: Sarah Lemas
Indexer: Ted Laux
Cover Photographer: Michael Lamotte
Photo Art Direction: Ingalls + Associates
Cover Design: Archer Design
Cover Captures: Guy Hart-Davis

Screen reproductions produced with Collage Plus.
Collage Plus is a trademark of Inner Media Inc.

SYBEX is a registered trademark of SYBEX Inc.

TRADEMARKS: SYBEX has attempted throughout this book to distinguish proprietary trademarks from descriptive terms by following the capitalization style used by the manufacturer.

SYBEX is not affiliated with any manufacturer.

Every effort has been made to supply complete and accurate information. However, SYBEX assumes no responsibility for its use, nor for any infringement of the intellectual property rights of third parties which would result from such use.

Library of Congress Card Number: 93-86589
ISBN: 0-7821-1400-8

Manufactured in the United States of America
10 9 8 7 6 5 4 3 2 1

To James A. Dienes

Acknowledgments

Many thanks to the people who contributed to the production of this book. In particular, thanks to: developmental editor Sarah Wadsworth for her patience and encouragement; editor Guy Hart-Davis for his extremely helpful suggestions; technical editor Erik Ingenito for his careful and complete review; and to typesetter Len Gilbert, artist Suzanne Albertson, and proofreader Sarah Lemas for their hard work.

A very special thanks to Sharon Crawford and David Krassner for providing invaluable advice and support.

Table of Contents

Introduction

xvii

Part One

New Features

1

New Features in Word 6.0 for Windows   2

Part Two

Command Reference

7

Alignment	8
Annotation	10
AutoCorrect	13
AutoFormat	16
AutoText	20
Binding Offset	23
Bookmarks	24
Borders and Shading	27
Bullets and Numbering	30
Captions	33
Change Case	36
Charts	38

Columns	39
Cross-Reference	42
Cut, Copy, and Paste	45
Database	46
Date and Time	49
Display	50
Document	52
Document Protection	55
Drag and Drop	58
Draw	59
Dropped Capital	62
Envelope	64
Exit	67
Field Codes	67
File Conversion	70
File Management	72
Find and Replace	81
Font	85
Footnotes and Endnotes	89
Forms	94
Frames	99
Go To	103
Grammar	103
Graphics	105
Headers and Footers	108

Help	112
Hidden Text	113
Hyphenation	115
Indent	117
Index	119
Insert File	124
Insert/Overtype	125
Keep Text Together	126
Keyboard	127
Labels	129
Language	132
Line Numbering	133
Line Spacing	135
Links	137
Macros	142
Mail	145
Mail Merge	147
Margins	152
Master Document	155
Menu	160
Numbering Headings	163
Object Linking and Embedding	164
Open	167
Outline	169
Page Break	172

Page Numbering 173

Page Setup 175

Paragraphs 177

Print 178

Print Preview 181

Print Setup 183

Repaginate 184

Repeat 184

Revisions 185

Ruler 188

Save/Save As 189

Section Layout 191

Select 193

Sort 195

Spelling 196

Spike 201

Startup Preferences 202

Status Bar 203

Style Gallery 204

Styles 206

Summary Info 211

Symbol 212

Table of Authorities 213

Table of Contents 217

Table of Figures 219

Tables	221
Tabs	231
Template	232
Tip of the Day	235
Thesaurus	236
Toolbar	237
Undo/Redo	239
Unit of Measurement	240
User Info	241
View	242
Watermark	243
Windows	244
Wizards	245
Zoom	246

Index

247

Introduction

Word 6.0 for Windows is a powerful word-processing program. Many new features have been added, and many regular features have been improved to help you complete your tasks more easily.

WHO NEEDS THIS BOOK?

Anyone upgrading from a previous version of Word for Windows or another word-processing application will find this book helpful and practical. If you are upgrading from Word 2.0 for Windows, this book will help you to easily compile your documents using Word's new or different commands. If you are upgrading from another word-processing application, use this book to quickly direct you step by step through each task necessary to write or enhance a document.

The command and feature entries and their associated tasks are listed concisely in alphabetical order. You can quickly find and read the information you need, then apply it to your task. The book fits easily in your briefcase or bag, or is small enough to be readily available on your desk.

CONVENTIONS USED IN THIS BOOK

Some experience using Windows and a mouse will help you understand the following terminology and conventions.

USING A MOUSE

These are the most important terms for using a mouse:

Click
: Point to an item, then press and release the left mouse button.

Double-click
: Point to an item and click twice in rapid succession.

Right click
: Point to an item, then press and release the right mouse button.

Drag
: Point to an item, then hold down the left mouse button while moving the mouse pointer and the item to a different location. Then release the mouse button.

Toolbar
: Point to a toolbar button or drop-down list box. The ToolTip for that item appears, to remind you of the button's function. Click on a button to carry out the command.

MENU COMMANDS

The following terms are used for menus and menu commands:

Menu
: Press **Alt** or **F10** to activate the menu bar. Then press the underlined letters to activate a specific command. Or click on the menu command, then click on the item in the drop-down menu list. Commands that have ellipses (…) display a dialog box with options you can select to carry out the command—for example, File ➤ Save… will produce the Save dialog box.

Shortcut menu
: Point to various items in Word and right click on an item. A shortcut menu of appropriate commands appears for the item. Click on the command you want to use, or press ↑ or ↓ to highlight the command, then press ↵.

Shortcut keys   Many commands on the menus have been assigned shortcut keys. Press the key sequence to carry out the command. Shortcut keys appear in parentheses beside the menu command in this book.

DIALOG BOXES

These are the main components of dialog boxes:

Text box   Type data in the box. Sometimes, you can adjust the data with attached spin wheels, or select an item from an attached list box.

Spin wheels   Spin wheels are small buttons attached to a text box, with upward- and downward-pointing triangles. Click on the appropriate button to adjust the selection in a text box. If the selection is a measurement, your adjustment will be in the default unit of measurement.

Drop-down list   Click on a drop-down list button (it has an underlined ↓ on it) to display the list, then click on an item in the list. Or press **Alt** and the underlined letter, then press ↓ to display the list. Use the ↓ and ↑ keys to highlight an item in the list, then press ↵ to select the item.

List box   Click on an item in a list box to select it. If there are more items in the box than can be displayed, a scroll bar appears on the right side of the list. You can scroll through the list to find the item you want. Or press **Alt**+ the underlined letter, then press ↓ to move the highlight into the list box, and use ↑ and ↓ to highlight the item in the list. Press ↵ to select the item.

Check box

Click on a check box or press **Alt**+ the underlined letter to select or clear the check box. When a check box is *selected,* an *X* appears in the box. A *cleared* check box is empty. You can select as many check box options as you wish in a dialog box.

Option button

Click on an option button or press **Alt**+ the underlined letter to select it. A *selected* option button is filled in with a black dot. You can select only one of a group of option buttons.

Command button

Three-dimensional buttons in dialog boxes are called *command buttons.* Click on a button or press **Alt**+ the underlined letter to carry out the command or display another dialog box.

Browse button

Some dialog boxes contain Browse buttons so you can select a different file or path.

Preview

A sample of the options you have selected appears in the Preview area of a dialog box. Each time you select a different option, the sample is updated to reflect your selection. If a large item is being previewed, a scroll bar may appear in the Preview area.

Description

The definition of an item you have selected appears in the Description area of some dialog boxes.

STYLISTIC AND TYPOGRAPHICAL CONVENTIONS

For concision and clarity, this book uses ➤ to separate choices in a series of menu options. For example, *select File ➤ Open* means that you should select File from the main menu (the list of options across the top of the screen), then select the Open option from the pull-down menu that appears.

This book uses underline to indicate the hotkeys on Word's menus. For example, to select <u>F</u>ile ➤ <u>O</u>pen, you could hold down the Alt key and press *F* and then *O*.

Words that appear in bold lettering indicate a key to press, for example **Alt** or **Del**, or a toolbar button to click, such as **Cut** or **Paste**.

Part One

New Features

NEW FEATURES IN WORD 6.0 FOR WINDOWS

Word 6.0 for Windows has many new or improved commands and features. The following new features make Word easier than ever to use.

Annotation	If you have a sound board, you can now add a sound annotation to a document. If you also have a microphone, you can add a voice annotation.
AutoCorrect	You can create an abbreviation for text you often use or correct words you often misspell with AutoCorrect entries. The entries are expanded or corrected when typed followed by a space or ↵ in your document.
AutoFormat	You can use AutoFormat to automatically apply uniform styles to the text of a document.
AutoText	You can insert an AutoText entry (formerly called a *glossary* entry) you have created in your document by selecting the AutoText button on the Standard toolbar or Edit ➤ AutoText.
Callout	If you want to add a callout to a chart, graphic, or document text, you can easily create and format the callout right in your document, using tools on the Drawing toolbar.
Captions	Word's new Captions feature allows you to automatically add numbered and labeled captions to graphics, charts, tables, and equations in your documents.

Change Case	Now you can change the case of selected text without applying a different format to the characters. For example, if you select a word to which S<u>m</u>all Caps format has been applied, you can select <u>T</u>itle Case to change the first letter of each word to regular uppercase.
Columns	You can now select one of the predefined column settings in the Columns dialog box, including columns of unequal width.
Cross-reference	The Cross-reference feature is much easier to use. You can type introductory text, select the type of reference you want and the item you want to reference, all without leaving the dialog box. Then you can mark the rest of the cross-references in your document.
Database	You can now insert a database from a Word document or from another application, and filter and sort the records you insert in your Word document.
Dialog Boxes	Word's new dialog boxes have tabs that allow you to change various options for commands and features without having to leave the dialog box. The dialog boxes now appear three-dimensional.
Display	There are several new display features, including a vertical ruler in Page Layout view, a Master Document view, and even the capability to remove all the menus, toolbars, and the status bar from your screen in Full Screen view.

Document Protection	Word 6.0 for Windows allows you to protect a document with a password so that the document text cannot be altered. You can protect a document so that only annotations can be added, only revisions will appear on the screen, or only form fields can be filled in.
Draw	You can use the Drawing tools to draw an object right in your document window. You can also insert text objects and callouts, insert a picture, or add a frame.
Dropped Capital	You can easily add dropped-capital formatting to the first letter or word of a paragraph, or size a graphic that is inserted at the beginning of a paragraph by using Format ➤ Drop Cap.
Envelope	You can now add a POSTNET Bar Code to the delivery address on an envelope, so the envelope can be automatically processed by the Post Office. If you do, you can also add an FIM-A or FIM-C bar code, which are bar codes that identify the front of the envelope for the Post Office's processing machines.
File Conversion	You can choose the specific options you want when you convert files created in different applications.
File Management	You can save search specifications for later use, and rebuild the list of files found. Find File has a new, easier-to-use format.
Font	Word's Character command is now called "Font." You can change all of the character formats in the Font dialog box.
Format Painter	You can use Format Painter to copy a format to one location or to several locations, rather than individually reformatting text.

Forms	You can use form fields to easily create and fill out online forms. You can protect the text of the form from any changes while allowing changes to the form fields.
Headers and Footers	You can easily create Headers and Footers by using the Header and Footer toolbar.
Help	Help is now available on the Standard toolbar, and includes Examples and Demos on how to use Word features.
Labels	You can add a POSTNET bar code to mailing labels, and easily select or create labels to print.
Macros	Macros are now easier to record and easier to assign to a toolbar, menu, or shortcut key sequence.
Mail	You can send electronic mail to others who have compatible mail or fax applications.
Mail Merge	Creating and merging a data source and a main document has never been easier than with the new Mail Merge Helper.
Master Document	Word's new master document view allows you to create a long master document with subdocuments for easier organization and management.
Numbering Headings	You can automatically number document headings to which you have applied one of Word's built-in heading styles.
Organizer	The Organizer lets you easily copy templates to existing documents or other templates, and to copy macros, AutoText entries, and toolbars to other templates.
Status Bar	The status bar now displays the function of a command or toolbar button, and you can double-click on corresponding sections to enter various modes, including overtype, revision marking, or macro recording.

Style Gallery	You can use the Style Gallery to copy styles from a template to an existing document.
Table of Authorities	You can now mark citations in legal documents, then automatically compile a table of authorities.
Table of Figures	You can create a table of figures using captions and labels you inserted or styles you applied.
Tip of the Day	Each time you start Word, the Tip of the Day dialog box appears with a useful tip on improving your efficiency in Word, or a humorous tip for living well. (Don't worry—you can turn Tip of the Day off.)
Toolbars	Word now has toolbars for almost every feature, which you can display or hide as you work in a document. Each toolbar button contains a ToolTip describing its function.
Undo/Redo	You can undo your last several actions using the Undo drop-down list on the Standard toolbar. To undo an action you "undid," choose Redo or select the action on the Redo drop-down list.
Revisions	You can merge revisions from different reviewers into an original document, or compare versions of a document to mark revisions made in the later version.
Watermark	You can create a drawing or text object, or insert a graphic into a header or footer so it will appear as a watermark on each page of a document.
Wizards	Word's new Wizards help you create documents using specific templates. Wizards ask you how you want your document to appear, then set it up according to options you choose.

Part Two

Command Reference

ALIGNMENT

You can align text in your document both horizontally (as in a left-aligned or justified paragraph) and vertically (as in the title on a title page).

To Align a Paragraph Horizontally

1. Position the insertion point into the paragraph you want to realign.

2. Choose Format ➤ Paragraph.

3. On the Indents and Spacing tab, choose one of the options in the Alignment drop-down list.

4. Select OK in the Paragraph dialog box.

You can also use the alignment buttons on the Formatting Toolbar or the alignment shortcut keys to change the alignment of selected text or text at the position of the insertion point.

 **OPTIONS**

Left (Ctrl+L)	Aligns paragraphs along the left paragraph indent or margin. (Text along the right edge is ragged.)
Centered (Ctrl+E)	Centers text between the left and right margins.
Right (Ctrl+R)	Aligns text along the right paragraph indent or margin. (Text along the left edge is ragged.)
Justified (Ctrl+J)	Aligns text along both the right and left indents or margins

To Align Text Vertically on a Page

To center text vertically on a page, first divide your document into sections. You can insert a section break anywhere in your document.

1. Put the cursor just after the text you want to include in a section and select Insert ➤ Break. Make sure Page Break is selected.

2. In the Section Breaks area of the Break dialog box, select Next Page to begin the new section on the next page.

3. Select OK in the Break dialog box.

4. Move the cursor above the section break, then select File Page Setup.

5. Click on the Layout tab to activate it.

6. Select an option in the Vertical Alignment drop-down list. The options are discussed below.

7. Select OK in the Page Setup dialog box.

OPTIONS

Top   Aligns the top line of text along the top margin.

Center   Centers paragraphs between the top and bottom margins.

Justified   Aligns text along both the top and bottom margins.

NOTES   To align just one line of text, make sure that the line is a separate paragraph. To align the last line of a justified paragraph or a short line of text that ends with a ↵, press **Shift+↵** at the end of the text.

See Also *Borders and Shading; Page Break; Page Setup; Paragraphs; Section Layout; View*

ANNOTATION

You can add notes and comments to a document with <u>I</u>nsert ►<u>A</u>n-notation. Text comments are formatted as hidden text and are marked with the initials of their writer (entered in the User Info dialog box). If you have a sound board and a microphone, you can also record and listen to voice annotations.

To Add a Text Annotation

1. Select the text or move the insertion point to the end of the text where you want to insert a comment.

2. Select <u>I</u>nsert ► <u>A</u>nnotation. A hidden annotation mark containing the number of the annotation and the initials of its writer is inserted in the document, and the annotation pane opens at the bottom of your screen.

3. Type your comment text. Format it if you wish.

4. To switch between the annotation pane and the document window, press **F6** or click in the document window or annotation pane.

5. When you are finished, close the annotation pane by pressing **Alt+Shift+C** or clicking <u>C</u>lose.

To Add a Voice Annotation

To insert an annotation that is both text and voice, insert the text annotation first. Then move the insertion point just after the annotation mark and add the voice annotation.

1. Select the text or move the insertion point to the end of the text where you want to insert a comment.

2. Choose <u>I</u>nsert ► <u>A</u>nnotation. The annotation mark is inserted in the document, and the annotation pane opens at the bottom of your screen.

3. Click the Insert Sound Object button in the annotation pane.

4. Record your annotation. (Check the sound board's documentation for instructions on recording a sound object.)

5. When you are finished in the annotation pane, click Close (**Alt+Shift+C**).

To Change an Annotation into Document Text

1. Double-click the annotation mark or select View ➤ Annotations.

2. Select only the text of the annotation in the annotation pane—do not select the annotation mark and paragraph mark at the end of the annotation.

3. Choose Edit ➤ Cut (**Ctrl+X**) to cut the text to the Clipboard.

4. Position the insertion point where you want to paste the annotation text, and then choose Edit ➤ Paste (**Ctrl+V**).

5. Delete the annotation mark in the document.

To Copy an Annotation

1. Select the annotation mark in the document window that you want to copy and choose Edit ➤ Copy (**Ctrl+C**). Alternatively, triple-click the annotation mark.

2. Move the insertion point to where you want to paste the annotation, and choose Edit ➤ Paste (**Ctrl+V**). When you paste the annotation, it and all subsequent annotation marks are automatically renumbered.

To Delete an Annotation

1. Select the annotation mark for the annotation you want to delete.

2. Press **Del** or choose <u>E</u>dit ➤ Cu<u>t</u> (**Ctrl+X**). All subsequent annotation marks are renumbered automatically. If you de- lete only the annotation text, the annotation mark will re- main in the document.

To Display or Hide Annotation Marks

1. Choose <u>T</u>ools ➤ <u>O</u>ptions.

2. In the Nonprinting Characters area of the View tab, select the Hi<u>d</u>den Text check box to display annotation marks; clear it to hide them.

3. Select OK in the Options dialog box.

You can also click the **Show/Hide ¶** button on the Standard toolbar or select <u>V</u>iew ➤ <u>A</u>nnotations to display annotation marks in the active document. To hide the marks, click the **Show/Hide ¶** button or select <u>V</u>iew <u>A</u>nnotations again.

To Print Annotations

To print a document and its annotations:

1. Select <u>F</u>ile ➤ <u>P</u>rint (**Ctrl+P**).

2. Choose <u>O</u>ptions.

3. In the Include with Document area, select <u>A</u>nnotations.

4. Click OK in the Options dialog box, and again in the Print dialog box.

To print only the annotations:

1. Choose <u>F</u>ile ➤ <u>P</u>rint (**Ctrl+P**).

2. Select Annotations from the <u>P</u>rint What drop-down list.

3. Select OK in the Print dialog box.

To Play Back a Voice Annotation

1. Select the <u>V</u>iew ➤ <u>A</u>nnotations.

2. Double-click the sound symbol (a button with a picture of a cassette tape) in the annotation pane.

To View a Text Annotation

1. If necessary, click the **Show/Hide ¶** button on the Standard toolbar to display hidden text.

2. Double-click the annotation mark you want to view, or select <u>V</u>iew ➤ <u>A</u>nnotations.

3. If necessary, select the <u>F</u>rom drop-down list and highlight the name of the reviewer whose comments you want to view.

4. Press **Alt+Shift+C** or click <u>C</u>lose to close the annotation pane.

NOTES You can edit text in the annotation pane when the pane is active. You can edit text in the document window when the window is active. Word automatically renumbers annotation marks whenever you add, copy, or delete an annotation.

See Also *Document Protection; Go To; Print; Revisions; Select; Undo*

N E W

AUTOCORRECT

With AutoCorrect, you can abbreviate entries for a logo, a phrase, or a word you often misspell and correct punctuation and spelling errors in your documents automatically.

To Automatically Correct Typing Errors

Select <u>T</u>ools ➤ <u>A</u>utoCorrect and select the appropriate check boxes in the AutoCorrect dialog box, then choose OK in the AutoCorrect dialog box.

 OPTIONS

Change 'Straight <u>Q</u>uotes' to 'Smart Quotes'	Replaces straight quotation marks with curly quotation marks.
Correct TWo INitial <u>C</u>Apitals	Changes the second capital letter in a word to lowercase.
Capitalize First Letter of <u>S</u>entences	Capitalizes the first letter after a period.
Capitalize <u>N</u>ames of Days	Changes the lowercase first letter in the name of a day to uppercase.

To Create an Entry

Each entry you create must have a unique name. The name you create can contain up to 31 characters, but it cannot contain any spaces. If you use a word as an entry, add a character or symbol to the abbreviation so AutoCorrect will not replace a real word in your document with an entry. The replacement item can contain as many as 255 characters.

1. To create an entry using an item in your document, select the item.

2. Select <u>T</u>ools ➤ <u>A</u>utoCorrect. The AutoCorrect dialog box appears, with a list of the entries that come with Word.

3. Make sure Replace <u>T</u>ext As You Type is selected.

4. Type an abbreviation in the R<u>e</u>place text box.

5. Type the text which you want to use as a replacement for the abbreviation in the With text box. If you selected an item in your document, it already appears in the With text box.

6. Plain Text is selected by default for a typed or selected entry. To include the formatting of an item you selected, select Formatted Text.

7. Select Add to add the entry to the list.

8. Select OK in the AutoCorrect dialog box.

To Delete an Entry

1. Choose Tools ➤ AutoCorrect.

2. Highlight the entry in the list you want to delete.

3. Select Delete.

4. Select OK to close the AutoCorrect dialog box.

To Edit an Entry or Abbreviation

1. Select Tools ➤ AutoCorrect.

2. Make sure Replace Text As You Type is selected.

3. Highlight the entry you want to edit in the list. Both the abbreviation and the entry appear in the Replace and With text boxes.

4. To edit the abbreviation, select it in the Replace text box and then select Delete. Type in the new abbreviation and select Add.

5. To edit the entry, select it in the With text box. Make the changes you want to the selected item, then select Replace. Select Yes to redefine an entry for an abbreviation already in the list.

6. Choose OK in the AutoCorrect dialog box.

To edit an entry or abbreviation for an item you selected in your document:

1. Make the changes to the entry in your document and then select the item.

2. Select Tools ➤ AutoCorrect.

3. Type an abbreviation in the Replace text box. If it is a new abbreviation, select Add. If the abbreviation is currently in use, select Replace, and then select Yes to confirm the replacement.

4. Choose OK in the AutoCorrect dialog box.

NOTES If you do not want Word to replace abbreviations with their assigned entries, clear the Replace Text as You Type check box in the AutoCorrect dialog box, then select OK.

See Also *AutoText; Spelling*

The AutoFormat feature automatically applies uniform styles and formatting to a document and improves its appearance. Review the changes AutoFormat makes, and either accept or reject them.

Word's templates come with many styles, such as headings, bulleted lists, and body text, already built in. Only text formatted with Normal or Body Text style is changed by AutoFormat. If you want AutoFormat to apply your own styles, you must redefine the styles built into Word.

To Format Text Automatically

1. Place the insertion point anywhere in a document to format the entire document, or select the text to format.

2. Choose Format ➤ AutoFormat. The AutoFormat dialog box appears.

3. Select OK to format the document automatically. The status bar displays the progress of the AutoFormat.

4. When the format is complete, the AutoFormat dialog box reappears with the options listed below.

 **OPTIONS**

Review Changes	Review and reject the changes AutoFormat made.
Style Gallery	Copy styles from a different document template.
Accept	Accept all the remaining changes applied by AutoFormat.
Reject All	Cancel all the changes AutoFormat applied to styles in the document.

To automatically format your document and accept all the changes in one quick step, select the **AutoFormat** button on the Standard toolbar.

To Review Changes Made by AutoFormat

When you select AutoFormat's Review Changes option, revision marks temporarily appear in your document. If you have a color monitor, they appear in color as follows:

- Blue paragraph marks indicate a style automatically applied to the paragraph.

- Red paragraph marks show a paragraph mark deleted.

- A red strikethrough character indicates deleted text or spaces.

- A blue underline character under text indicates an added underline.

- Change bars in the margin indicate any line where formatting changes have taken place.

You can suppress the display of the revision marks by selecting Hide Marks in the Review AutoFormat Changes dialog box.

1. After the AutoFormat, select Review Changes in the Auto-Format dialog box. The Review AutoFormat Changes dialog box appears.

2. Use the scroll bars to scroll through the document and review the changes. Or select ← Find to highlight the previous change and Find → to highlight the next change in the document. If the dialog box is in the way, drag its title bar to a different location on your screen.

3. To change the style of selected text, click on the Style drop-down list and select another style in the list. Hold down **Shift** while you click on the Style drop-down list on the Formatting toolbar to see a list of all available styles.

4. Select the appropriate option, described below, for each change you want to revise.

5. When you have finished reviewing and revising changes, select Close in the Review AutoFormat dialog box.

6. In the AutoFormat dialog box, choose Accept to accept all the changes you didn't revise, or Reject All to reject all the changes made by AutoFormat.

To Set AutoFormat Options

You can select the elements of the document to which Word applies styles. You can also manage some other changes AutoFormat makes to the text, such as replacing extra paragraph marks and spaces with paragraph formats that include spacing.

1. Select Tools ➤ Options, and click on the AutoFormat tab. Or select Format ➤ AutoFormat and select Options.

2. Select or clear the options you want AutoFormat to manage. By default, all the options are selected.

3. Choose OK in the Options dialog box. If you are returned to the AutoFormat dialog box, select OK to format the document with the selected options or Cancel to return to the document window.

 **OPTIONS**

Preserve	Select Previously Applied Styles to keep styles you have applied to selected text.
Apply Styles To	Select Headings to automatically apply heading styles to headings in your document. Select Lists to automatically apply bullets, numbers, and multilevel formats to lists in your document. Any bullets or numbers already in the lists are replaced with the new format. Select Other Paragraphs to apply formatting to paragraphs other than headings and lists.
Adjust	Select the Adjust area check boxes to add needed or remove extra Paragraph Marks or Tabs and Spaces, and to remove Empty Paragraphs between some paragraph styles.
Replace	Select Straight Quotes with Smart Quotes to replace regular quotation marks with curly marks. Select Symbol Characters with Symbols to replace (C), (R), and (TM) with ©, ®, and ™. Select Bullet Characters with Bullets to automatically replace the first character in a list item, such as an asterisk, with bullets or numbers your printer can print.

NOTES To view a list of styles in the current document, click on the Styles drop-down list on the Formatting toolbar. Character styles appear in normal text; paragraph styles appear bold.

See Also *Font; Paragraphs; Status Bar; Style Gallery; Styles; Template*

AutoText lets you quickly insert entries you have saved in a document. You can create named entries for text or graphics that you use often, such as the return address or closing of a letter. AutoText was called the Glossary in previous versions of Word.

To Create an AutoText Entry

AutoText entry names can contain as many as 32 characters and can include spaces.

1. Select the item you want to save as an AutoText entry. To save the item's format, make sure you also select its paragraph mark (¶).

2. Click the **AutoText** button on the Standard toolbar, or select <u>E</u>dit ➤ AutoTe<u>x</u>t. The AutoText dialog box appears.

3. If you want, type a new name for the entry in the <u>N</u>ame text box.

4. If necessary, select the <u>M</u>ake AutoText Entry Available To drop-down list and select the name of the document template where the entry will be saved. By default, entries are saved in the NORMAL.DOT template.

5. Select <u>A</u>dd in the AutoText dialog box.

To Delete an Entry

1. Select Edit ➤ AutoText.

2. Highlight the name of the AutoText entry in the Name list box.

3. Select Delete, then select Close.

To Edit an Entry

1. Insert the entry in your document. Make the desired changes to the entry.

2. Select the entry, including the paragraph mark if you want to save the entry's formatting.

3. Click on the **AutoText** button on the Standard toolbar, or select Edit ➤ AutoText.

4. Highlight the name of the entry in the Name list box.

5. Select the Add button, then select Yes to redefine the name you selected.

To Edit a Name

1. Choose Format ➤ Style.

2. Select the Organizer button and then select the AutoText tab.

3. Highlight the name you want to change in the In NOR-MAL.DOT list box and choose Rename. The Rename dialog box appears.

4. Type the name you want to change the selected name to, and choose OK.

5. Choose Close in the Organizer dialog box to return to your document.

To Insert an Entry

1.   Move the insertion point to where you want to place the AutoText entry.

2.   Choose Edit ➤ AutoText.

3.   Highlight the name of the entry in the Name list box.

4.   To insert the entry with its formatting, select Formatted Text. To insert the entry so that it will be formatted like the text preceding it, select Plain Text.

5.   Select Insert.

You can also insert an entry using the keyboard and the AutoText toolbar button. Type several letters of the entry's name and click the AutoText button on the Standard toolbar. The entry is inserted in the position of the insertion point.

To Print a List of Entries

You can print a list of the AutoText entries and their contents that are attached to the current document. The entries are printed in alphabetical order by name, and the contents are printed in their original format. Template entries are printed first, followed by entries stored in NORMAL.DOT, and then any entries stored in add-in templates.

1.   With the document whose AutoText entries you want to print active, choose File ➤ Print (**Ctrl+P**).

2.   Select the Print What drop-down list and highlight AutoText Entries in the list.

3.   Choose OK in the Print dialog box.

NOTES   Select the space or punctuation after a phrase you want to use as an entry so that when you insert it in a document, the space or punctuation will also be inserted.

If you don't know where you want to store an entry, specify the NORMAL.DOT template so the entry will be available to all documents, regardless of which template they are based on.

You can insert an AUTOTEXT field code instead of a defined entry, then use the **F9** (Update) key to change all occurrences of the same entry in a document when you edit the entry.

 **See Also** *AutoCorrect, Field Codes*

BINDING OFFSET

You can print a document so that extra space is allowed on the edge where the document will be bound. This extra space is called a *binding offset* or *gutter margin*. The binding offset can be along the left edge of all pages, or you can set up mirror margins so the binding offset will alternate between the inside and outside margins of documents that will be printed on both sides of the paper.

To Add a Binding Offset

1. Choose File ➤ Page Setup. If necessary, click the Margins tab.

2. To add a binding offset to the left margin only, go to step 3. To add a binding offset to facing pages, select the Mirror Margins check box. The Left and Right margin text boxes change to Inside and Outside respectively.

3. Type a measurement in the Gutter text box, or click on the spin buttons to adjust the measurement.

4. In the Apply To drop-down list, select This Section, This Point Forward, or Whole Document.

5. Select OK in the Page Setup dialog box.

NOTES   Use File ➤ Print Preview to see how your document will look after adding a binding offset.

See Also   *Margins; Page Setup*

BOOKMARKS

Use bookmarks to name a selection or location in your document. You can then move quickly to the location, calculate numbers, mark pages for an index entry, or create cross-references in your document.

To Create a Bookmark

Bookmark names can be as long as 40 characters, must begin with a letter, and can contain numbers. You cannot include spaces in a bookmark name, but you can use the underline (_) character.

1.   Select the text or item, or move the insertion point to the place in your document where you want to insert a bookmark.

2.   Choose Edit ➤ Bookmark (**Ctrl+Shift+F5**).

3.   Type a name for the bookmark in the Bookmark Name text box.

4.   Select Add to add the bookmark to the list box.

To Delete a Bookmark

To delete a bookmark in your document:

• If you assign a bookmark name that is already in the document to a new bookmark, the previous bookmark with that name is deleted.

- Select <u>E</u>dit ➤ <u>B</u>ookmark, highlight the name of the book-mark you want to delete, and select <u>D</u>elete to delete the bookmark but leave its marked text in the document.

- Select the bookmark bracket and its marked text then press Backspace or **Del** to delete the bookmark and its marked text.

To Display Bookmarks

When you display a bookmark in a document, it will appear as a pair of square gray brackets for selected text or as a large insertion point for a location in the current document.

1. Choose <u>T</u>ools ➤ <u>O</u>ptions and select the View tab.

2. In the Show area, select the Boo<u>k</u>marks check box.

3. Select OK in the Options dialog box.

To hide the bookmarks in your document, clear the Boo<u>k</u>marks check box in the Options dialog box.

To Edit a Bookmark

You can cut or copy a bookmark and paste it into another location in the current document or into another document. You can delete part of a bookmark, or add text to a bookmark in your document.

- When you copy a bookmark or part of a bookmark to a lo-cation in the same document, only the text or item is cop-ied, not the actual bookmark.

- When you cut a bookmark and paste it in a location in the same document, the text or item and the bookmark move to the new location.

- If you copy a bookmark and paste it in another document, both documents will have the same bookmark. If the other document already has a bookmark with that name assigned, the bookmark will not be pasted into the document. The original bookmark will retain its name and location.

- If you delete part of a bookmark, the undeleted portion of the item stays marked.

- You can add text between any two characters in a bookmark. The text you add will become part of the bookmark.

- To add text at the beginning of a bookmark, add the new text just before the marked text.

- To add text at the end of bookmark text, type the text, then select all the text and the bookmark brackets. Choose Edit ➤ Bookmark, then choose Add.

To Move to a Bookmark

1. Select Edit ➤ Bookmark.

2. Highlight the name of the bookmark you want to go to, and select Go To. If the bookmark is a location, the insertion point will move to the location. If the bookmark is selected text, the text will be selected when you move to it.

3. When you have finished locating the bookmarks you are looking for, select Close.

By default, the Name option button is selected so bookmarks are listed in alphabetical order in the Bookmark Name list box. Select Location if you want to sort the bookmark names in the order of their locations.

You can also use Edit ➤ Go To (**F5**) to move to a bookmark.

To Perform Calculations

1. Assign a bookmark name to each number in your document that you want to include in the calculation.

2. Move the insertion point to where you want the result of your calculation to appear.

3. Select Insert ➤ Field. The Field dialog box appears. By default, the =(Formula) field is selected.

4. Type the formula in the Field Codes text box. Use the assigned bookmark name for each number in the calculation.

5. Select OK in the Field dialog box.

If you change any of the numbers in the document, position the insertion point just after the number and press Backspace. Do not select the number and type over the selection because it will delete the bookmark and render your calculation meaningless.

👁 **See Also** *Cross Reference; Cut, Copy, and Paste; Field Codes; Go To*

BORDERS AND SHADING

By using the Borders toolbar or Format ➤ Borders and Shading, you can add borders and shading to a selected paragraph or a selected item, whether it is regular document text, text in a cell or frame, or even the actual cell or frame.

To apply a border or shading to a paragraph, select only the paragraph, even if it is in a cell or a frame. To apply a border or shading to a table cell, including its contents, select the cell and the end-of-cell mark. To apply a border to a graphic or frame, or shading to a frame, select the graphic or frame.

To Apply Custom Borders and Shading

1. Select the paragraph or item.

2. Choose Format ➤ Borders and Shading. The Paragraph Borders and Shading dialog box appears.

3. To apply and customize a border, select the Borders tab, and choose from the options described below.

4. To apply and customize the shading, select the Shading tab, and choose from the options below.

5. Select OK in the Paragraph Borders and Shading dialog box.

OPTIONS The options on the Borders tab of the Paragraph Borders and Shading dialog box are as follows:

Presets	Select None, Box, or Shadow as the border around your selection.
Border	The Border area displays the preset border option you have selected. Or you can click on the position in the Border area where you want to add or remove a border. The positions are top, bottom, left, right, inside, outside, or no borders.
From Text	Enter the amount of space in points between the borders and the paragraph.
Line	Select None to remove selected borders from the side of a paragraph, cell, graphic, or frame or select a line format in the Style list box.
Color	Select the color for the border. You must have a color monitor to display the border in the color you selected. If you have a color printer, the border will print in the selected color.

The options on the Shading tab of the Paragraph Borders and Shading dialog box are as follows:

None	Removes all shading from the selection.
Custom	Applies the selected shading pattern and colors to the selection.

Shading   Select a shading density or pattern to
                   apply to the selection.

Foreground   Choose the foreground color for a pattern
                   you have applied to the selection.

Background   Choose the background color for a pattern
                   you have applied to the selection.

To Apply Predefined Borders and Shading

Use the Borders toolbar to apply predefined borders or shading to
a paragraph, table cell, or frame. To display the Borders toolbar,
click on the **Borders** button on the Formatting toolbar or choose
Show Toolbar in the Paragraph Borders and Shading dialog box.

1. Select the paragraph or item to which you want to apply a
   border or shading.

2. To apply a border, select the Line Style drop-down list to
   display the list of line styles. Highlight the line style you
   want to use, then click on one of the border formatting
   buttons on the Borders toolbar. You can select a top, bottom, left, or right border, inside or outside border, or no
   border to remove a border.

3. To apply shading, select the Shading drop-down list and highlight the amount of shading or the shading pattern in the list.

4. Click in the document window to deselect the text or item.
   The borders and shading you chose appear around the
   items you selected.

 NOTES   Borders and shading you apply to a paragraph
extend between the paragraph indents. You can adjust the width of
bordered or shaded paragraphs by adjusting the indentation.

⊙ **See Also**   *Frames; Graphics; Indent; Paragraphs; Ruler*

BULLETS AND NUMBERING

Use Format ➤ Bullets and Numbering to create a bulleted or numbered list automatically. You can also apply a multilevel format that includes both bullets and numbers.

To Add Bullets, Numbers, or a Multilevel List

1. Select the list text, or move the insertion point where you want to begin a bulleted or numbered list.

2. Select Format ➤ Bullets and Numbering and then select the Bulleted, Numbered, or Multilevel tab. Select one of the samples on the tab, and then click OK in the Bullets and Numbering dialog box. Or click on the Numbering or Bullets button on the Formatting toolbar to add bullets or numbers to the selection.

To remove bullets or numbers from a list or list item, select the list or item and click on the Bullets or Numbering button, or click the right mouse button and select Stop Numbering. Alternatively, select the list or item, choose Format ➤ Bullets and Numbering, and select Remove. Word will automatically update numbering for remaining numbered list items.

To Change Items in the List

- To stop bullets or numbers in a list, move the insertion point to the position in the list, click the right mouse button, and select Skip Numbering.

- To add a new item to the list, move the insertion point to a position just before the location where you want to insert an item, then press ↵. Then type the item.

- To paste into the list an item you have cut or copied to the Clipboard, move the insertion point to the position just before the location where you want to paste the item and

press ⏎. Then click the **Paste** button on the Standard toolbar or select Edit ➤ Paste (**Ctrl+V**).

• To rearrange the text of the list alphabetically, numerically, or
by date, select the list items and choose Table ➤ Sort Text.

Numbering for the list will automatically update when you make
changes to your list.

To Modify the List Format

You can change the appearance of the list by changing the text before or after a bullet or number, or by changing the bullet symbol,
the way the bullets or numbers are aligned, or the space between
the bullet or number and an item in the list.

1. Select the list text whose bullet or number format you
want to change.

2. Choose Format ➤ Bullets and Numbering, or right-click
the list and choose Bullets and Numbering.

3. Select the tab for the type of list you want to change. If necessary, select one of the formats on the tab.

4. Select Modify. The Modify *type* List dialog box appears.

5. Change the necessary options, described below, to refor-
mat the bullets or numbers in the selection.

6. Choose OK.

 **OPTIONS**

Bullet Character Select the type of bullet you want in the
predefined bullet formats. Or select the
Bullet button, choose a symbol you
want to use for a bullet, then select OK.
You can also type or adjust the Point
Size, or select the Color drop-down list
and choose the color of the bullet.

Number Format	In the Number Format area of the Modify Numbered List and Modify Multilevel List dialog boxes, type the Text Before and the Text After the number or bullet in the corresponding text box. Select the format of the Bullet or Number from the drop-down list. Select Font to change the font, font size, and special effects applied to the number or bullet. Type or adjust the Start At number for the list. In the Modify Multilevel List dialog box, select the Include from Previous Level drop-down list and choose Nothing, Numbers, or Numbers and Position for each level except the first. Choose the Level *Number* from the scroll box.
Bullet Position or Number Position	Choose Left, Centered, or Right from the Alignment of List Text drop-down list. Enter the Distance from Indent to Text and the Distance from Bullet to Text or the Distance from Number to Text. Select Hanging Indent to apply a hanging indent to the list text.

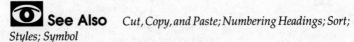

NOTES   Text you type in the Text Before and the Text After text boxes when modifying a numbered or multilevel list cannot contain more than 32 characters or be longer than one line. Use the Decrease Indent or Increase Indent buttons on the Formatting toolbar to promote or demote multilevel list items. Define a style for a modified list format you want to save.

See Also   *Cut, Copy, and Paste; Numbering Headings; Sort; Styles; Symbol*

NEW

CAPTIONS

Word's new Caption feature allows you to easily add a caption to a selected item or to all items of the same type in your document. Captions are added as field codes. All the captions in your document are automatically updated when you add or delete a captioned item.

To Add Captions Automatically

Use the AutoCaption feature when you create a document that will contain items to which you want to add a caption. Captions inserted after you "turn on" the AutoCaption feature will be uniformly formatted and correctly numbered.

You can add more than one type of caption to your document. For each type of caption you add automatically, select a specific label and caption position.

To add text to the caption after it is inserted in your document, place the insertion point after the caption label and type the text.

1. Position the insertion point in your document where you want to begin automatically adding captions. Then select Insert ➤ Caption.

2. Select AutoCaption in the Caption dialog box. The Auto-Caption dialog box appears.

3. Select the check box beside the item you want to add captions to in the Add Caption When Inserting list box.

4. Select the label for the item in the Use Label drop-down list. Or select the New Label button, type a name for the label in the Label text box, and choose OK in the New Label dialog box.

5. Choose Above Item or Below Item in the Position drop-down list.

6. If you want to change the format of the caption numbering, select Numbering and then choose the number format and appearance you want. See *To Modify the Caption Format* below for additional information.

7. Repeat steps 3–6 for each item you want to add a caption to automatically.

8. Choose OK in the AutoCaption dialog box.

Once you have made AutoCaption selections for a document, Word asks when you exit if you want to save global template changes. Choose Yes if you want your AutoCaption selections available for all new documents.

To Add Captions Manually

Use Insert ➤ Caption to add a caption to a selected item in your document.

1. Select the item to which you want to add a caption.

2. Choose Insert ➤ Caption. The Caption dialog box appears, with the label and caption number for the item.

3. Select any of the options described below.

4. Choose OK in the Caption dialog box.

 **OPTIONS**

Caption — Type the text for the caption in the text box. You cannot type over the label and caption number that automatically appear in the text box.

Label — Choose Equation, Figure, or Table from the drop-down list. The label you choose appears in the Caption text box.

Position	Choose Above Selected Item or Below Selected Item in the drop-down list as the place where the caption will appear.
Numbering	Displays the Caption Numbering dialog box. Select the Format drop-down list, then select a format in the list to change the number format for specific label types. If you want the chapter included in the numbering, select the Include Chapter Number check box. You can then select a style from the Chapter Starts with Style drop-down list, and the separator character to use between the chapter number and the number of the captioned item from the Use Separator drop-down list. Choose OK in the Caption Numbering dialog box.
New Label	Type a name for the label in the Label text box and select OK.
Delete Label	Select a label name you have defined, then choose Delete to delete the label name. The label will not be deleted from items it is assigned to in your document, but it will no longer be available for additional items to which you want to add a caption.
AutoCaption	Turns on AutoCaption.

To Edit Captions and Labels

Once you have added a caption, either automatically or manually, you can easily edit the text you added to the caption using the regular editing techniques.

You can also edit the caption for a single label or for all the labels of a specific type. However, you cannot change the label or number of a caption by typing over it.

1. Select the caption with the label you want to change.

2. To change a single caption's label, delete the caption by pressing **Backspace** or **Del.**

3. Select Insert ➤ Caption.

4. Select a different label in the Label drop-down list. Or select New Label, type a label in the Label text box, and choose OK in the New Label dialog box.

5. Choose OK in the Caption dialog box.

To Modify the Caption Format

You can change the default formats of both the caption's numbering and paragraph style in your document. The format for all captions of the same type will be changed in your document.

1. Select a caption of the type whose numbering format you want to change and choose Insert ➤ Caption.

2. Select Numbering, and fill in the options in the Caption Numbering dialog box. The options are described above.

3. Choose OK in the Caption Numbering dialog box, and again in the Caption dialog box.

👁 **See Also**   *Draw; Field Codes; Graphics; Tables; Template*

You can change the case of selected text with Format ➤ Change Case. Or press **Shift+F3** to cycle through the capitalization options.

1. Select the text whose case you want to change.

2. Choose Format ➤ Change Case. The Change Case dialog box appears.

3. Select one of the options (described below) in the dialog box.

4. Choose OK.

 **OPTIONS**

Sentence Case	Capitalizes the first letter of the first word at the beginning of a sentence, or the first letter of the first word after a sentence.
lowercase	Changes selected text to lowercase letters.
UPPERCASE	Changes the selected text to uppercase letters
Title Case	Capitalizes the first letter of each selected word.
tOGGLE cASE	Changes uppercase to lowercase and lowercase to uppercase in the selection.

 **NOTES**   When you change the case of selected text, you are not applying new formatting to it. To apply a new format to selected text, choose Format ➤ Font and then select All Caps or Small Caps as the effect. If a smaller-size capital font is available, you can print small caps.

The Change Case command does not affect text you select that already has the small caps format. Remove the format if you want to change the text to lowercase letters.

See Also   *Font*

CHARTS

Use Microsoft Graph to create a visual representation of the data in a Word table or spreadsheet, or enter your data directly into Graph's datasheet. You can also import data from another application to create a chart with Graph.

The Microsoft Graph window contains two windows of its own—the Chart window and the Datasheet window. Use commands on Graph's Window menu to switch between the chart and the datasheet window, or to change the size of the chart window.

To Create a Chart

1. Select the table data you want to chart, or move the insertion point to the location in your document where you want the chart to appear.

2. Click the **Insert Chart** button on the Standard toolbar. Or select Insert ➤ Object, choose Microsoft Graph from the Object Type list box on the Create New tab, and select OK. You can also use File ➤ Import Data to import data created with another application, or File ➤ Open Microsoft Excel Chart to import a chart created with Excel.

3. If necessary, select the Datasheet window and replace the sample data in each cell.

4. Select File ➤ Exit and Return to *document* to close Graph and embed the chart in your document.

To Edit the Chart

When the chart window is active, you can edit and format chart items or the entire chart. You can change the type of chart, add text or arrows, change the colors of chart items, and add patterns to chart items you select. The changes you make appear immediately in the chart window.

To select an item in the chart, click on the item or press the arrow keys to cycle through chart items. Click just inside the chart window to deselect chart items.

The datasheet is a spreadsheet used for entering and formatting chart data. When the datasheet is active, edit the cell contents or format the data in the datasheet.

To Embed the Chart in a Document

Use File ➤ Update to send to your document changes you make in the chart while you remain in Graph for further editing.

When you are finished editing and formatting the chart, select File ➤ Exit and Return to *document* to embed the chart as an object in your document. Save your document to save the chart.

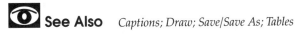 **See Also**   *Captions; Draw; Save/Save As; Tables*

N E W

COLUMNS

You can add newspaper columns to a document or part of a document. Newspaper columns are columns that let text flow from the bottom of one column to the top of the next.

Columns can be of equal or unequal width. When you insert columns in a document, you can format the whole document in multiple columns, or automatically add a section break to the portion of the document you want to make columnar.

To view columns in your document, you must be in Page Layout or Print Preview.

To Add Columns to a Document

1. Move the insertion point to the position in your document where you want to place columns.

2. Select Format ➤ Columns. The Columns dialog box appears.

3. Select a column definition from the Presets area of the dialog box.

4. Choose the Apply To drop-down list, and select the portion of the document that you want to be columnar.

5. Choose OK in the Column dialog box.

To add columns of equal width, use the **Columns** button on the Standard toolbar. Position the insertion point anywhere in the document and click on the **Columns** button to apply column format to the entire document. Or select the text you want to make columnar and click the **Columns** button to apply columns to the selection.

To Edit Document Columns

You can edit some column features using the horizontal Ruler, shortcut keys, or commands from the menu bar.

- Drag the left or right column marker to change the widths of all columns of equal width, or to change only the column whose marker you are adjusting in columns of unequal width.

- Drag the indent marker to align it with the column marker to remove indents from paragraphs in a column.

- You can also select the indented paragraph in columnar text, choose Format ➤ Paragraph, and change the indent options to 0.

- Place the insertion point where you want to insert a column break, then press **Ctrl+Shift+↵** to start a new column.

- Place the insertion point where you want to insert a column break, then select Insert ➤ Break. Select Column Break, then choose OK in the Break dialog box.

- To balance the lengths of columns on a page, move the insertion point to the end of the column you want to balance
and choose Insert ➤ Break. Select Continuous, then
choose OK in the Break dialog box.

Use the options in the Columns dialog box to specify exact measurements for your column format.

To edit columns in your document, move the insertion point anywhere in the columns and select Format ➤ Columns. Change the
necessary options, described below, to format your columns as you
want them to appear, then choose OK in the Columns dialog box.

 **OPTIONS**

Presets	Select One, Two, or Three as the number of equal columns, or Left or Right as the position of the smaller column in columns of unequal widths.
Number of Columns	Type or adjust the number of columns you want at the location of the insertion point.
Width and Spacing	Type or adjust the Spacing for the first column in columns of equal width. If you have defined columns of unequal width, type or adjust the Width of the column or the Spacing between columns for each Col # you want to change.
Equal Column Width	Formats the columns with equal width. Clear the check box for columns of unequal width.
Apply To	Select the drop-down list, then highlight Whole Document to apply column format to the document or section, or select This Point Forward to apply column format from the position of the insertion point to the end of the document or section.

Line Between	Adds a line between the columns.
Start New Column	Adds a column break at the location of the insertion point.

🗞 **NOTES**   Insert a table when you want to create side-by-side paragraphs in a document such as a fax cover sheet.

You can add graphics to columnar text. You can position a graphic in a frame so that it is in one column, part of a column, or across several columns.

👁 **See Also**   *Forms; Frames; Graphics; Keep Text Together; Paragraphs; Ruler; Section Layout; Tables*

CROSS-REFERENCE

Use cross-references to refer your reader to additional or related information in a different part of the same or a different document. You can create cross-references to heading text formatted with a heading style, footnotes and endnotes created with Insert ➤ Footnote, captions created with Insert ➤ Caption, and bookmarks created with Edit ➤ Bookmark. Cross-references are inserted as field codes, and are especially useful in long documents such as master documents.

To Create Cross-References

1.   Position the insertion point where you want to create a cross-reference, and then type any introductory text, such as *See Page*. Be sure to insert a space after the introductory text.

2.   Select Insert ➤ Cross-reference. The Cross-reference dialog box appears.

3. Highlight the type of item you want to cite in the Reference Type list box. You can select Heading, Bookmark, Footnote, Endnote, Equation, Figure, Table, or a caption label you created as the type of reference.

4. Highlight the type of information about the item that you want to place in your document in the Insert Reference To list box. Your choices in the list box depend on the type of reference you selected in step 3. (See *Options* below.)

5. Choose the item you want to refer to in the For Which *Item* list box.

6. Select Insert.

7. Click in the document window to activate it, then insert any optional text or the new introductory text for the next cross-reference. Repeat steps 3–5 to create each additional cross-reference.

8. Select Close to return to your document when you have finished creating cross-references.

OPTIONS

Heading Text	Inserts the text you have specified if it is formatted as a Heading style.
Heading Number	Inserts the heading number applied with Format ➤ Heading Numbering.
Page Number	Inserts the number of the page where the cross-reference item is located.
Paragraph Number	Inserts the number of the paragraph, applied with Format ➤ Bullets and Numbering, where a bookmark is located.
Bookmark Text	Inserts the text of a defined bookmark.
Footnote Number	Inserts the reference number of a footnote.

Endnote Number	Inserts the reference number of an endnote.
Entire Caption	Inserts the label, number, and optional text of a caption.
Only Label and Number	Inserts the caption's label and number, but not the optional text.
Only Caption Text	Inserts the optional text of a caption, but not the caption's label and number.

To Edit a Cross-reference

- Select the introductory or optional text you want to edit, and type the new text. The text you type replaces the selection.

- When you delete an item you have cited, an error message appears the next time you update the cross-reference.

- To delete a reference placed in the document by Word, select the reference and press **Backspace** or **Del**.

- To change a reference placed in the document by Word to a different type of reference, select the reference and choose Insert ➤ Cross-reference. Choose a different item from the Insert Reference To list box, and then choose Insert.

NOTES   To insert cross-references in a different document, make sure both documents are included in a master document.

You can include section or chapter cross-references in a Header or Footer by applying a Heading style to the section or chapter in the document, and then inserting the heading text as a cross-reference in the Header or Footer text.

See Also   *Bookmarks; Captions; Field Codes; Footnotes and Endnotes; Numbering Headings; Master Document; Styles*

CUT, COPY, & PASTE

Use the Edit menu or the Standard toolbar to cut or copy text, tables, graphics, charts, or any item in your document to the Clipboard. You can then paste the item into the same document or another document, or even into a document in another application.

To Cut or Copy an Item

When you click the **Cut** button or select Edit ➤ Cut (**Ctrl+X**), you remove the selected item from your document and place it on the Clipboard. When you click the **Copy** button or select Edit ➤ Copy (**Ctrl+C**), the selection remains in the document and a copy is placed on the Clipboard.

1. Select the item to move or copy.

2. Choose Edit ➤ Cut (**Ctrl+X**) or click the **Cut** button on the Standard toolbar to move the selection, or Edit ➤ Copy (**Ctrl+C**) or the **Copy** button on the Standard toolbar to copy the selection to the Clipboard.

To Paste an Item into a Document

Once you have placed an item on the Clipboard, whether you have cut it or copied it from your document, use Edit ➤ Paste (**Ctrl+V**) or click the **Paste** button on the Standard toolbar to place it in the location you want in your document.

NOTES   The contents of the Clipboard can be pasted into a document as many times as you wish. However, each time you cut or copy a selection to the Clipboard, the Clipboard contents are replaced with the current selection.

 **See Also**   *Drag and Drop; Spike*

N E W

DATABASE

You can easily insert an existing database or some other source of data, such as the data in a spreadsheet, into a Word document. With Insert ➤ Database, you can select which fields of data you want from the data source and filter the selection of records to be inserted in a table in your document. You can also format the table to meet your needs and have Word update the table if the data source changes.

Word can insert Excel and Access files, and can convert many other types of files. You can also filter and insert records from a Word database, such as a merge data source file, into another Word document.

To Insert a Database in a Document

1.   Move the insertion point where you want the database to appear in your document.

2.   Select Insert ➤ Database. The Database dialog box appears.

3.   Select Get Data. The Open Data Source dialog box appears.

4.   Select the name of the file you want to use as the data source in the File Name list box and choose OK. If necessary, select OK in the *Application Name* dialog box that appears.

5.   If necessary, select Query Options to insert and sort specific information from the data source. Select the query options (described below) you want to use in the Query Options dialog box, then select OK.

6.   Select Table AutoFormat and highlight the name of the table format you want to use in the Formats list box. Select any other option to apply to the table format in the Table AutoFormat dialog box, then select OK. The Table Auto-Format options are described below.

7.   Select Insert Data. Choose the options (described below) you want in the Insert Data dialog box, then select OK. The database is inserted into your document.

 **OPTIONS**   Options in the Query Options dialog box are as follows:

Filter Records   Select the Field drop-down list, and highlight the data source field you want to use in the comparison. Select the Comparison drop-down list, and highlight the operator you want to use for alphabetic and numerical data. Type the alphabetic or numerical value you want to compare with the field you selected in the Compare To text box. To include more fields, operators, and comparison values, select the And/Or drop-down list. Choose And if additional criteria must be met in the filter; choose Or if only one of the criteria should be met. To erase all the selection criteria and insert all the data source records, select Clear All.

Sort Records   Choose the Sort By drop-down list, then highlight the field you want as your first data selection in the inserted table. Select Ascending (a-z) or Descending (z-a) to define the alphabetical or numeric order of the items in the table. If necessary, choose Then By for the second and third fields, and choose Ascending or Descending for each.

Select Fields   All the fields are listed in the Fields In Data Source list box. Fields to be included are listed in the Selected Fields list box. Highlight a field in the Selected Fields list box and choose Remove to eliminate the field in the table. Choose Remove All to eliminate all the fields from appearing in the table. If you highlight a field in the Fields In Data Source list box, choose Select to add the field to the Selected Fields list box. Choose Select All to include all the data source fields in the table. Select the Include Field Names check box to use the field names as column names in the table. To remove all the field selection criteria, choose Clear All.

The Table AutoFormat options are as follows:

Formats   Highlight the name of the predefined format in the list box, or select *(none)* to remove all borders and shading. You can also use the Borders and Shading command or toolbar to customize the format of your table.

Formats to Apply   Select the Borders, Shading, Font, and/or Color check boxes to apply the defined formats in the predefined format you selected for the table. Select the AutoFit check box to adjust the table size according to how much text you chose to insert.

Apply Special Formats To   You can select Heading Rows, First Column, Last Row, and/or Last Column as the database items to which you apply special formats.

The Insert Data dialog box options are as follows:

<u>A</u>ll	Inserts all the records that meet the selection criteria. If no selection criteria are specified, all the records are inserted.
<u>F</u>rom	Selects a range beginning with the record in the text box.
<u>T</u>o	Type the last record you want to include in the range in the text box.
<u>I</u>nsert Data As Field	Inserts the specified source data as a database field. When inserted as a field in your document, you can update changes made to the data source in a Word document.

NOTES   You can search for the file you want to use as a data source with <u>F</u>ind File in the Open Data Source dialog box. See "File Management" for information on performing and saving a search.

If you insert the database as a field in your document, each time you update the database you will lose any table formatting you have applied to the table. To update a database with a selected table format, you must reinsert the database and the table format in your document. If you edit a table inserted as a Database field, your changes will be lost when you next update the field.

See Also   *Field Codes; File Management*

DATE AND TIME

You can insert your system's date and time into a document as either text or a field code. If you insert the date or time as text, it will stay the same as when it was inserted in your document. If you insert the date or time as a field code, you can update the field to reflect the current system date and time.

To Insert the Date and Time

1. Move the insertion point to the location where you want to insert the date or time.

2. Select Insert ➤ Date and Time. The Date and Time dialog box appears.

3. Highlight the date or time format you want to place in your document in the Available Formats list box.

4. To enter the date or time as a field code, select Insert as Field. Clear the check box to enter the date or time as text.

5. Choose OK in the Date and Time dialog box.

 **See Also** *Field Codes*

N E W

DISPLAY

By default, Word displays several screen elements, including the title bar, menu bar, status bar, and toolbars. You can control the display of screen elements and characters that do not print, such as paragraph marks and tabs, for all your documents. Some new features in Word 6.0 for Windows include options to allow three dimensional dialog boxes and to change the background and text colors.

To Change the Display Defaults

1. Select Tools ➤ Options, and select the View or the General tab in the Options dialog box. The default options for the current view are displayed on the View tab.

2. Select the check box of any option you want to display.
Clear the check box of any option you do not want to
show on your screen. The options are described below.

3. Choose OK in the Options dialog box.

OPTIONS   The options available on the View tab depend on the view of the current document.

Show	Displays Drawings or Draft Font, Object Anchors or Wrap to Window, Text Boundaries, Picture Placeholders, Field Codes, and Bookmarks. Select the Field Shading drop-down list to choose when to apply shading to a field code.
Window	Displays the Status Bar, Horizontal Scroll Bar, Vertical Scroll Bar, and Vertical Ruler. In Normal view, adjust the Style Area Width measurement.
Nonprinting Characters	Select Tab Characters, Spaces, Paragraph Marks, Optional Hyphens, or Hidden Text, or select All to display all the nonprinting characters in the document window.

You can also click the **Show/Hide ¶** button on the Standard toolbar to
display all the nonprinting characters in your document window.

Display options on the General tab of the Options dialog box are:

Blue Background, White Text	Displays document windows with white text on a blue background.
3D Dialog and Display Effects	Displays dialog boxes and screen elements as three-dimensional objects.

See Also   *Bookmarks; Field Codes; Hidden Text; Menu;
Ruler; Toolbar; View*

DOCUMENT

You can have several documents open at the same time in Word. The exact number depends on the amount of memory you have in your system.

To Close the Current Document

To close the active document without exiting Word.

1. Select File ➤ Close.

2. If you made any changes to the document since it was last saved, a dialog box will appear asking if you want to save your changes. Select Yes to save the changes, No to close without saving the changes, or Cancel to keep the document open.

To Move Through a Document

You can move through your document using the keyboard or the mouse. The insertion point, which appears as a blinking vertical line on your screen, shows where the character you type next will appear. The mouse pointer appears as an I beam. You cannot move beyond the last character in the document.

Table 2.1 shows various ways you can move around your document.

To Open a New Document

Each time you start Word, a new, blank document window appears. You can immediately begin entering text in the Normal style in the document window. There are several ways you can open a new, blank document window whenever you want while you are working in Word.

To quickly open a document that is based on the NORMAL.DOT template:

• Click on the **New** button on the Standard toolbar.

Table II.1: Various ways to move around your document

To Move To	Press This Key	Click with the Mouse
Character left	←	—
Character right	→	—
Line up	↑	up scroll button
Line down	↓	down scroll button
Word left	Ctrl+←	—
Word right	Ctrl+→	—
End of line	End	right scroll button
Beginning of line	Home	left scroll button
Beginning of paragraph	Ctrl+↑	—
Beginning of next paragraph	Ctrl+↓	—
Up one screen	Page Up	above the scroll box
Down one screen	Page Down	below the scroll box
Top of screen	Ctrl+Page Up	—
Top of previous page	Alt+Ctrl+Page Up	—
Top of next page	Alt+Ctrl+Page Down	—
Beginning of document	Ctrl+Home	drag scroll box
End of document	Ctrl+End	drag scroll box
Same position of previous page (in Page Layout view)	—	Previous Page button
Same position on next page (in Page Layout view)	—	Next Page button

Table II.1: Various ways to move around your document (continued)

To Move To	Press This Key	Click with the Mouse
Last edit location (even in another document)	Shift+F5	—
Second-to-last edit location (even in another document)	Shift+F5, Shift+F5	—
Third-to-last edit location (even in another document)	Shift+F5, Shift+F5, Shift+F5	—

- Select File ➤ New and choose OK.

- Press **Ctrl+N.**

To open a new document that is based on a different template or that uses a document Wizard, use the following steps:

1. Select File ➤ New. The New dialog box appears.

2. Highlight the name of the template or Wizard you want to base the document on in the Template list box.

3. In the New area of the dialog box, make certain that Document is selected.

4. Optionally, select Summary and enter the summary information for the file you are creating.

5. Select OK in the New dialog box.

NOTES A tab, space entered with the Spacebar, and ↵ are all considered characters by Word.

Use commands on the Window menu to switch the full screen display between different open documents. You can also resize your document windows to display more than one open document at a time.

 **See Also**   *Exit; Open; Save/Save As; Summary Info; Template; Windows; Wizards*

DOCUMENT PROTECTION

You can protect the text of a document from being changed by others, assign a password to the file, or assign a write reservation password to the document.

Passwords are case sensitive. They can contain as many as 15 characters made up of numbers, letters, symbols, and spaces.

To Assign or Edit a Write Reservation or Protection Password

When you assign a Write Reservation Password to a document, anyone who doesn't know the password can open the document only as read-only. No changes made to it will be saved when it is read-only.

To protect a document from any changes at all—including revisions, annotations, or filling in form fields—set a Protection Password for the file. Only a person who knows the password can open the document. You must save a file with a protection password before the protection goes into effect.

You can change the write reservation password only in a file that was not opened with read-only status.

1. Activate the file you want to protect or whose password you want to edit, select File ➤ Save As, and then select Options. The Options dialog box appears with the Save tab selected. Or choose Tools ➤ Options and select the Save tab.

2. To protect the document, type a password in the Write Reservation Password or the Protection Password text box in the File Sharing Options for *document* area of the Save tab. The characters you type appear as asterisks. To edit an existing password, highlight the asterisks, then type the new password in the text box.

3. Select OK in the Options dialog box. The Confirm Password dialog box appears.

4. Type the password again in the Reenter Write Reservation/Protection Password text box, then select OK in the Confirm Password dialog box.

5. If necessary, choose OK in the Save As dialog box. If you used Tools ➤ Options to set the password protection, select File ➤ Save or click the **Save** button on the Standard toolbar to activate the password protection.

To remove a write reservation password, highlight the asterisks in the Write Reservation Password text box and press **Del**. Then save the file. If you opened the file as Read Only, you cannot save the original file. Instead, save the file to a new name.

To Protect the Document's Text

If you don't want others to revise your document, you can protect the text of the document or a section of your document with a password. Only a person who knows the password can change the text of a protected document. However, others can add annotations or revision marks to a protected document, or fill in fields in a protected form.

1. Choose Tools ➤ Protect Document. The Protect Document dialog box appears.

2. Select one of the options described below.

3. Type the password in the Password text box. An asterisk appears for each character you type.

4. Choose OK in the Protect Document dialog box. The Confirm Password dialog box appears.

5. Type the password again in the Reenter Protection Password text box, then choose OK in the Confirm Password dialog box. The document text is now protected from any changes.

To turn off the text protection of a document. Choose Tools ➤ Unprotect Document. The Unprotect Document dialog box appears. Type the assigned password in the text box, and choose OK.

 **OPTIONS**

Revisions | Follow revisions made to the document by others. Revisions cannot be accepted or rejected and reviewers cannot turn off revision marking. Any changes made are marked as revisions.

Annotations | Reviewers can insert annotations, but cannot change the document contents.

Forms | Allows users to fill in the form fields, but not change any of the form's text. Then, if necessary, select Sections. The Protected Sections list box contains a list of the sections in your document. Clear the check box beside each section in the list box that you do not want to protect, then choose OK in the Section Protection dialog box.

 **NOTES** You can also recommend that a document be opened as read-only by selecting the Read-Only Recommended check box in the Options dialog box. When this is selected, a dialog box appears each time the file is opened asking whether to open the file as read-only. If the user opens the file as read-only, no changes can be saved.

See Also *Annotations; Forms; Revisions; Save/Save As*

DRAG AND DROP

Use Word's Drag-and-Drop feature to move or copy text, graphics, or any document item within a document or to another document. Drag and Drop is useful for moving or copying items a short distance from the selection.

When you are dragging and dropping a document item, the mouse pointer appears with a small box that has a gray dotted border, and the insertion point appears as a dotted gray vertical line.

To Move or Copy

1. Select the document item you want to move or copy.

2. Drag the selection to a new location to move it. Hold down **Ctrl** while you drag the selection to copy it.

3. Release the mouse button.

To Select the Drag-and-Drop Feature

To use Drag and Drop, make sure it is selected.

1. Select <u>T</u>ools ➤ <u>O</u>ptions and choose the Edit tab in the Options dialog box.

2. Select <u>D</u>rag-and-Drop Text Editing in the Editing Options area of the tab. Clear the check box to turn off Drag and Drop.

3. Select OK.

NOTES   You cannot drag and drop an item anywhere off the screen. To drag to another document, arrange the two documents side by side on your screen. To move or copy an item a farther distance, use the **Cut, Copy,** and **Paste** commands or toolbar buttons.

 **See Also**   *Cut, Copy, and Paste*

You can use Microsoft Draw to create a drawing in a document. Draw is easier to use than it was in previous versions of Word, and now can add callouts to graphics.

To draw or see drawings in your document, you must be in Page Layout or Print Preview.

To Create a Drawing

1. Click the **Drawing** button on the Standard toolbar. The Drawing toolbar appears just above the Status Bar. Or click the right mouse button on a displayed toolbar and select Drawing on the shortcut menu.

2. Optionally, click on the **Create Picture** or the **Insert Frame** button to place a picture in your document at a specified location.

3. Click on one of the Drawing tools—Line, Rectange, Ellipse, Arc, or Freeform—to draw an object.

4. Move the mouse pointer into the document, picture, or frame. The mouse pointer appears as a small cross when you are using one of the drawing tools.

5. Drag the mouse pointer in the window to draw the object. When you release the mouse button (except for freeforms), the object is complete.

If you make a mistake and want to cancel a drawing (except for a freeform), press **Esc** while you are still holding down the mouse button. Or select the object and press **Del** to delete it after it has been drawn.

You can copy an object by holding down **Ctrl** while you drag the copy of the object to a different location.

To Create a Text Object

You can place text in a text box when you want to position text in front of or behind document text. You can import a graphic into a text box, and then position it in relation to the document text. For example, a watermark would be placed behind the text of the document in a text box.

Selected text in the text box can be formatted with the regular formatting commands. However, the text box will not expand to include all your text as a frame will. You must size the text box and position the text in it with the Size and Position tab in the Drawing Object dialog box. You can also resize the text box by dragging one of its handles inward to make the text box smaller or outward to make it larger, or by dragging the margin markers on the horizontal and vertical Ruler bars.

To create a text object:

1. Click on the **Text Box** tool, then drag in the window to create a text box. The text box appears as a rectangle with a paragraph mark in it.

2. If necessary, choose the font format you want for the text in the text box.

3. Type the text you want in the text box, or choose Insert ➤ Picture to insert a graphic in the text box.

4. To adjust the size of the text box and position of the text or graphic in it, choose Format ➤ Drawing Object or right-click on the border of the text box and choose Format Drawing Object. The Drawing Object dialog box appears.

5. Choose the Size and Position Tab.

6. Adjust the Position, Size, and Internal Margin as necessary.

7. Choose OK in the Drawing Object dialog box.

To Edit a Drawing

Once you have created a drawing or imported a vector drawing, you can change any of its parts using tools on the Drawing toolbar or Format ➤ Drawing Object.

Select the part of the object to edit, then change the fill color or pattern, line color, and line style. Change the order of objects by sending objects to the front or back of other objects or document text. Group or ungroup multiple selections. Change the position of an object by moving or copying it, flipping it horizontally or vertically, rotating the object to the right, or aligning objects along a grid relative to another object or the page. Change the shape of a freeform or the size of an object or group.

To Insert and Format a Callout

Use a callout to tie a text object to a graphic. Draw lets you insert and format a callout in your document.

1. Click the **Callout** button on the Drawing toolbar.

2. Move the mouse pointer to where you want the callout line to begin, then drag to form the line with an attached text box for your text.

3. Type the text you want in the callout text box.

4. To change the format of the callout, select the callout and then click the **Format Callout** button. The Format Callout dialog box appears.

5. Select the appearance for your callout in the Type area of the dialog box.

6. Choose any of the formatting options to format your callout.

7. Select OK in the Format Callout dialog box.

To Select Drawing Objects

•   Click on the object or group you want to select.

- Click on the Select Drawing Objects button on the Drawing toolbar, then drag to create a rectangle that surrounds the object or group.

- If an object has no fill, click on its lines.

- To select multiple objects or groups, hold down Shift while you click the objects.

- To cancel a selection, click in a blank area of the doucment window, or press Shift while you click the object or group.

Selected objects appear with small black squares, called *handles*, around them.

 **NOTES**   To use the same drawing tool several times, double-click on it when you select it on the Drawing toolbar. To draw an object outward from its center, click on the drawing tool and then hold down **Ctrl** while you drag the mouse pointer.

Your drawings will not print when you are printing a Draft Output copy of your document.

See Also   *Fonts; Frames; Graphics; Watermark*

N E W

DROPPED CAPITAL

You can add dropped-capital formatting to a paragraph to make selected text at the beginning of the paragraph appear in a large, bold font. The selected text is placed in a frame, and the paragraph text wraps around the frame. Use scalable fonts such as TrueType, ATM, or PostScript fonts for the best results with dropped capitals.

To Create Dropped Capitals

1. Move the insertion point into the paragraph where you want a dropped capital letter, or select the first word of the paragraph.

2. Choose Format ➤ Drop Cap.

3. In the Position area of the Drop Cap dialog box, select Dropped to place the selection within the paragraph or In Margin to place the selection in the margin beside the top of the paragraph.

4. Optionally, select the Font drop-down list and choose a different font for the selection.

5. To change the height of the dropped capital letter, enter the number in the Lines to Drop text box.

6. Adjust the measurement in the Distance From Text box.

7. Choose OK in the Drop Cap dialog box. If you are in Normal view, Word asks if you want to change to Page Layout to see how the dropped capital appears in your document. Choose Yes.

To remove the dropped capital format from your paragraph, move the insertion point anywhere in the paragraph and choose Format ➤ Drop Cap. Select None in the Position area of the Drop Cap dialog box, then select OK.

NOTES You can apply borders and shading to the frame that surrounds the dropped capital. You cannot place a dropped cap in the margin of a columnar document.

To resize the height of a graphic at the beginning of a paragraph to a specific number of lines, select the graphic and then choose Format ➤ Drop Cap.

 **See Also** *Borders and Shading; Columns; Frames; Graphics*

Use Word's Envelope feature to quickly print an envelope for a document. Word will automatically insert the return and delivery addresses.

You can also mark the return and delivery addresses in your document with bookmarks recognized by Tools ➤ Envelopes and Labels. Use EnvelopeAddress as the bookmark name for the delivery address and EnvelopeReturn to mark the return address in a document that contains several addresses.

To Address and Print an Envelope

1. Select the mailing address if the document contains more than one address.

2. Choose Tools ➤ Envelopes and Labels, and, if necessary, select the Envelopes tab in the Envelopes and Labels dialog box.

3. If necessary, type a different return address in the Return Address text box.

4. Choose any other options necessary on the Envelopes tab. The options are described below.

OPTIONS The options on the Envelopes tab of the Envelopes and Labels dialog box are as follows:

Omit	Omits printing the return address.
Print	Select the button to print the envelope.

Add to Document	Adds a section that contains the envelope formatting to the beginning of a document. If you already have an envelope section in a document, the button changes to Change Document.
Feed	Displays how to place the envelope in the printer so the text will be correctly placed.
Options	Displays the Envelope Options tab and sets additional options for your envelope.

The options on the Envelope Options tab are as follows:

Envelope Size	Select the drop-down list, then highlight the definition of the envelope size you want to use. To create an envelope size that does not appear in the list, select Custom Size. The Envelope Size dialog box appears. Adjust or type the measurements in the Width and Height text boxes. Then select OK in the Envelope Size dialog box.
If Mailed In the USA	Select Delivery Point Bar Code to have Word automatically print the bar code of the delivery address's zip code. If you have selected the Delivery Point Bar Code check box, the FIM-A Courtesy Reply Mail check box is also available. Select it to print a facing identification mark to mark the front of a courtesy reply envelope.
Delivery Address/Return Address	Choose Font/Font to change the format of the font in the specified area. Select From Left/From Top to indicate the distance from the edge of the envelope. You can also change the style of both the delivery and return addresses in your document to change the font and reposition the text. Or you can move the delivery address (which is inside a frame) in your document if you added the envelope to it.

To Include Graphics on an Envelope

If you want to add special text or graphics to an envelope and use it each time you create an envelope based on the current template, save the text or graphic as an AutoText entry. Use Tools ➤ Envelopes and Labels to insert two AutoText envelope entries named EnvelopeExtra1 and EnvelopeExtra2.

1. Create the envelope using the steps and any necessary options described above. Then select the Add to Document or Change Document button.

2. Make sure you are in Page Layout view. Then type any special text, insert a graphic with Insert ➤ Picture, or create a drawing with the Drawing toolbar.

3. Adjust the position of the special text or graphic on your envelope. Place text that is not a text object and graphics you have inserted into a frame so each can be positioned on the envelope.

4. Select the text or graphic and choose Edit ➤ AutoText.

5. Type EnvelopeExtra1 or EnvelopeExtra2 in the Name text box, and select Add.

Delete the AutoText entry when you no longer want to use it for every envelope you print based on the template.

NOTES By default, Word inserts FIM-A codes when the check box is selected. To insert an FIM-C code for bulk mail, insert a BarCode field with the \f "C" switch.

See Also *AutoText; Field Codes; Font; Frames; Graphics; Labels; Styles; Template*

EXIT

Always exit correctly so that you don't lose your data when you exit Word for Windows. If any open documents have been changed, Word prompts you to save the changes for each. If a document has never been saved, the Save As dialog box appears. Type a name for the file in the File Name text box, then select OK.

There are several ways to exit from Word:

- Select File ➤ Exit.

- Double-click on the Control menu box.

- Click on the Control icon or press **Alt+Spacebar** to reveal the Control menu, then choose Close.

- Press **Alt+F4**.

 **See Also**   *Document; Save/Save As; Window*

FIELD CODES

Use field codes when you want Word to enter specific information automatically in your document. The uses of field codes include entering the date and time, individual page numbers, or the number of pages in a document, and marking entries for indexes, cross-references, and tables of contents.

Word supports more than 60 types of fields, which are referenced in the Programming Information section of Help Contents.

To Display Field Codes or Results in a Document

When you enter a field code in your document, its result is displayed rather than the actual code. You can toggle the display of a single selection between field codes and results.

1. Move the insertion point into the field.

2. Click the right mouse button to display the shortcut menu and select Toggle Field Codes. Or press **Shift+F9** to toggle the field code or **Alt+F9** to toggle all field codes in the document.

It is easier to see what information has been entered as a field code if you select a shading option for field codes in your documents. You can also change the display to view all the field codes in your document.

1. Select Tools ➤ Options and choose the View tab in the Options dialog box.

2. In the Show area of the tab, select the Field Shading drop-down list and choose the shading option.

3. Select Field Codes to display the codes. Clear the check box to display the results.

4. Select OK in the Options dialog box.

To Edit a Field Code

To edit a field code inserted in your document:

1. Move the insertion point into the field.

2. If necessary, toggle the results to display the field code.

3. Make any changes using regular editing techniques.

4. Press **Shift+F9** to display the field's results.

5. Press **F9** to update the field code.

To Format a Field Code

You can directly format the results of a field code in your document, although the formatting may be lost when you update the field. You can also add the appropriate format switch (*) to the field code instructions to format the field code results. Then when you update the field, the formatting will remain in the field results by default. There are case-conversion switches, number-conversion switches, and character-formatting switches you can use in your field code instructions.

To Insert a Field Code

A field code consists of field characters, which look like braces but cannot be entered using the brace keys, a field type, and the in-structions you enter. The instructions can be either required or optional, and may have optional switches.

You can type the field code and instructions in your document if you enter the field characters by pressing **Ctrl+F9**. However, it is easier and more efficient to use Insert ➤ Field.

1. Move the insertion point to where you want to enter the field code.

2. Choose Insert ➤ Field. The Field dialog box appears.

3. Select a field category in the Categories list box. If you want to see an alphabetical listing of all the field codes, highlight All in the list.

4. Select the field code you want to use in the Field Names list box. The name you select appears in the Field Codes text box.

5. Type the instructions for the field code after the name in the Field Codes text box. If necessary, select Options and choose the options you want for the field code, then select OK in the Field Options dialog box.

6. Make sure Preserve Formatting During Updates is selected.

7. Select OK in the Field dialog box.

To Update Fields

There are several procedures for updating fields:

• Select the field and press **F9** (Update).

- Select <u>E</u>dit ➤ Select A<u>l</u>l (**Ctrl+A**) to select the entire document, and then press **F9**. All the fields in the document will be updated.

- Move the cursor into the field and click the right mouse button. Select Update Field from the shortcut menu.

- To always update the field codes when you print your document, choose <u>T</u>ools ➤ <u>O</u>ptions and select the Print tab. In the Printing Options area, select the <u>U</u>pdate Fields check box. Then choose OK in the Options dialog box.

 **NOTES**   Press **Ctrl+F11** or **Ctrl+3** to lock a field. A locked field cannot be updated unless the original BOOKMARK, IN-CLUDETEXT, or REF field has been changed. Locked fields have the Lock Result (\!) switch added to the field code instructions. Press **Ctrl+Shift+F11** or **Ctrl+4** to unlock a field.

To select the next field in your document, press **F11**; to select the previous field, press **Shift+F11**. You can unlink a linked field and display its last results by pressing **Ctrl+Shift+F9** or **Ctrl+6**.

See Also   *Links; Object Linking and Embedding*

N E W

FILE CONVERSION

Word for Windows automatically converts many formats of files created with other applications when you open one of the files in Word. You can also save a Word file to one of several different file formats.

Word allows you to change some defaults so that it will resemble the behavior of another word processing application. No changes are made to the document, only to the way Word behaves with it. The compatibility options you select are saved with the document.

To Change the Compatibility Options

1. With the document whose compatibility you want to change active, select Tools ➤ Options and choose the Compatibility tab.

2. If necessary, select the Recommended Options For drop-down list, then highlight the name of the file's conversion application.

3. To substitute an available font for one in the document that is not available on your system, select Font Substitution. Select the options you want, then select OK to return to the Options dialog box. Font substitution options are described below.

4. To save the options you selected as the defaults in the current template, select Default, then select Yes. The defaults will be displayed in every document Word opens that is based on the template.

5. Choose OK in the Options dialog box.

OPTIONS   The following options are available in the Font Substitutions dialog box:

Font Substitutions	The Missing Document Font list displays the list of fonts in the document that are not available on your system. Highlight the name in the list for which you want to select a substitute. The name you select appears in the Missing Document Font area. The Substituted Font list displays a list of fonts with which you can replace the missing fonts.

Substituted Font	Choose a font in the drop-down list. The display in the document is changed to the substituted font. If Default is the selected substituted font, Word chooses the font on your system that most resembles the font in the document. The name of the default font is displayed in the area under the Substituted Font drop-down list.
Convert Permanently	Permanently replace the substituted fonts for the missing fonts in the document. If the file is later converted back to its original format, the substituted fonts will appear in the document.

NOTES   The substituted fonts are saved with your document, and are also saved in the MSFNTMAP.INI file in your Windows directory. If for some reason the substitutions in the document are different than those in the MSFNTMAP.INI file, the settings in the MSFNTMAP.INI file will override the settings in your document.

Use the EditConversionOptions macro to modify the length of lines or the way some fields are converted. Run the macro, then follow the instructions to change the file converter.

 See Also   *Graphics; Macros; Open; Save/Save As*

Use Word's Find File feature to locate a document by its name, key words, author, date, or specific words in the document. Information you enter in the Summary Info dialog box can also be used as the search criteria.

You can preview the found document or select multiple files to simultaneously open, delete, or print. You can even save the criteria you used for a search so you can use them again.

To Define or Change the Search Criteria

1. Select File ➤ Find File. The Search dialog box appears the first time you choose the command. If you have already saved a set of search criteria, the Find File dialog box appears. Select Search to display the Search dialog box.

2. To select a different set of search criteria, select the Saved Searches drop-down list and highlight a name. Go to step 9.

3. Highlight a name in the File Name drop-down list in the Search For area or type the name of the file or the * wildcard and the file extension in the text box. You can specify more than one file name or extension by typing a semicolon between each name or extension.

4. Select the drive letter to search in the Location drop-down list.

5. To save the specified search criteria, select Save Search As and type a name for the search in the Search Name text box. Then select OK in the Save Search As dialog box.

6. Optionally, select Rebuild File List to replace the previously found files with a new list that meets the criteria.

7. To include subdirectories of the drive letter in the Location text box, select the Include Subdirectories check box.

8. To place further restrictions on the search results, select Advanced Search to display the Advanced Search dialog box. Select the options you want and then choose OK. The dialog box options are described below.

9. Choose OK in the Search dialog box to begin the search.

OPTIONS   The remaining options in the Search dialog box are as follows:

Delete Search	Select a name in the Saved Searches drop-down list then choose the button to delete a named set of search criteria.
Clear	Empties all the search text boxes and check boxes so you can specify different search criteria.
Close	Closes the Search dialog box and return to the Find File dialog box.

The Advanced Search dialog box contains the following options on the Location tab:

File Name	Select the drop-down list and highlight a name, or type a name or the * wildcard and the extension of the types of files to search for in the text box. Indicate a search for multiple files or extensions by typing a semicolon between each in the text box.
Search In	The list box contains the list of directories that will be searched.
Directories	Highlight the directories you want to search in the list box.
Add	Add a highlighted directory in the Directories list box to the Search In list box.
Remove	Remove a highlighted directory from the Search In list box.
Remove All	Remove all the directories from the Search In list box.
Include Subdi-rectories	Searches all the subdirectories of the directories in the Search In list box.
Network	Displays the Network-Drive Connections dialog box.

The Advanced Search dialog box contains the following options on the Summary tab:

(Title, Author, Keywords, Subject)	Type information in any of the text boxes that matches information saved in the Summary Info dialog box of the file for which you are searching. You can specify approximate criteria to search for when you use special characters to indicate the criteria. Table II.2 shows the special characters that can be used to specify search criteria.
Options	Highlight one of the options in the drop-down list to define how the Listed Files in the Find File dialog box will be used in the search. The files in the list box may have been selected with a different set of criteria. Choose Add Matches to List to add the names of files that meet the search criteria to the current list. Choose Search Only in List to list only the files in the current list that match the specified criteria. Select Create New List to replace the current list with only the files that meet the criteria.
Match Case	Finds only files that contain the exact characters and case of the text in the Containing Text text box.
Containing Text	Enter text that is in a file you wish to find.
Use Pattern Matching	Uses advanced search criteria for the text in the Containing Text text box. Some of the special characters you can use appear in the Special pop-up list. Table II.3 contains a list of the advanced search criteria characters.

Special   In the pop-up list of special characters, highlight the character you want to use in the Containing Text text box.

The Advanced Search dialog box contains the following options on the Timestamp tab:

Last Saved   Type the earliest date in the range you want to search in the From text box, and the latest date in the To text box. (Leave the From text box empty to search for all files saved before the date in the To text box. Leave the To text box empty to search for all files saved after the date in the From text box.) Type the name of the last person who saved the document in the By text box.

Created   Type the earliest date in the range you want to search in the From text box, and the latest date in the To text box. (Leave the From text box empty to search for all files created before the date in the To text box. Leave the To text box empty to search for all files created after the date in the From text box.) Type the name of the document's creator in the By text box.

To Display File Information

After you have defined your search criteria and performed a search, the search results are displayed in the Listed Files list box of the Find File dialog box.

1. Highlight the file you want to see information about in the Listed Files list box. By default, the contents of the file are displayed in the Preview of *file name* list box.

2. In the Find File dialog box, select the View drop-down list.

Table II.2: Special characters for searching for documents

Special Character	Searches For	Example
?	a single character	**b?t** finds both *bat* and *bit*
*	any number of characters	**m*y** finds *merry, may,* and *my*
" "	the exact characters	**"Long hot summer"** finds *Long hot summer*
\	(makes special character a real character)	* finds a real asterisk
'	OR	**long,hot** finds documents containing either *long* or *hot*
& *or* space	AND	**long&hot** or **long hot** finds documents containing both *long* and *hot*
~	NOT	**~long** eliminates any document that contains *long*

3. Choose File Info to display file information such as the file's title, size, and last saved date. Or choose Summary to display the information entered into the file's Summary Info dialog box, and the file's statistics.

4. To define or select different search criteria, select S̲earch.

5. To open the selected file, choose O̲pen. To return to your current document, choose Close.

Table II.3: Advanced search characters you can use to search for
documents in Find File and for characters in Find and
Replace

Special Character	Searches For	Example
?	a single character	**b?t** finds both *bat* and *bit*
*	any number of characters	**m*y** finds *merry*, *may*, and *my*
\	(makes special character a real character)	***** finds a real asterisk
[]	any of the characters	**s[aei]t** finds *sat*, *set*, and *sit*
[-]	one character in the range (in ascending order)	**[m-s]eek** finds *meek*, *peek*, *reek*, and *seek*
[!]	one character other than the one in the brackets	**[!s]ore** finds *more* and *pore*, but not *sore*
[!m-n]	one character other than those in the range	**gr[!a-j]pe** finds *grope* but not *grape* or *gripe*
{n}	number of occurrences of previous	**me{2}t** finds *meet* but not *met*
{n,}	at least the number of occurrences of previous	**me{1,}t** finds *meet* and *met*
{n,m}	range of number of occurrences of previous	**50{1,4}** finds *50*, *500*, *5000*, and *50000*
@	one or more occurrences of previous	**me@t** finds *met* and *meet*
<	beginning of word	**<(derm)** finds *dermatologist* but not *pachyderm*

Table II.3: Advanced search characters you can use to search for documents in Find File and for characters in Find and Replace (continued)

Special Character	Searches For	Example
>	end of word	>(**derm**) finds *pachyderm* but not *dermatologist*
\num~	rearrange text in the Find What text box	(Clinton)(Bill) in the Find What text box and \2\1 in the Replace With text box to change *Clinton Bill* to *Bill Clinton*

To Manage Files in the List

1. Select File ➤ Find File. The Find File dialog box appears.

2. Select the file or files you want to use.

3. Choose Commands. A pop-up list of commands appears.

4. Select one of the commands in the list. A description of the commands appears in *Options*, below.

 **OPTIONS**

Open Read Only	Any selected files are opened as read-only. No changes can be saved.
Print	Opens the Print dialog box. Choose the options you want to use to print all the files in the selection, then choose OK.

Summary   Edit the summary information of the selected file, or the first file in a multiple selection.

Delete   Delete the selected files from your disk. Choose Yes in the confirmation dialog box to delete the files.

Copy   In the Copy dialog box, you can copy the files to an existing directory by typing the destination drive and directory in the Path text box. Or you can select the drive letter in the Drives drop-down list, then select the directory in the Directories list box. To create a new directory, select New and type the drive letter and new directory name in the Name text box, then select OK in the Create Directory dialog box. You can also select Network in the Copy dialog box to connect to a network drive. When you have selected your copy options, choose OK in the Copy dialog box.

Sorting   Select Sorting to display the Options dialog box and choose the sorting criteria for all the files in the Listed Files list box. In the Sort Files By area, select Author, Creation Date, Last Saved By, Last Saved Date, Name, or Size. The files are sorted alphabetically, chronologically, or from smallest to largest. In the List Files By area, choose Filename to display the file's name, or Title to display the file's title assigned in the Summary Info dialog box. If the file does not have an assigned title, the file is listed with its name between hyphens. When you have selected the sorting criteria, select OK.

To Select Files in the File List

You can select one file or several files to perform some operations, such as delete, print, or copy.

1. Select File ➤ Find File. The Find File dialog box appears.

2. Click on the first file name you want to select. Then hold down **Ctrl** while you click on any additional file names. Or, if you want to select a range of adjacent files, hold down **Shift** while you click on the last file in the range.

NOTES The search criteria you save are placed in the WINDOWS\FILEMAN.INI file. If you delete this file, all your saved searches will also be deleted.

You can print a file's summary information and statistics using options in the Print dialog box.

When you use the Copy command in Find File, make certain that each file in your selection is assigned a unique file name. You can use wildcards to indicate the names of files you copy.

See Also *Open; Print; Summary Info*

FIND AND REPLACE

Use Edit ➤ Find (**Ctrl+F**) to search for text, formatting, special characters, and other document items. Use Edit ➤ Replace (**Ctrl+H**) to both search for any of the document items and replace a found item with a specified item.

To Find Document Items

1. Select Edit ➤ Find (**Ctrl+F**). The Find dialog box appears.

2. Type the text you want to find in the Find What text box, or select the Find What drop-down list and highlight one of the items in the list. The last four items you have searched for appear in the list.

3. Select Search, then choose Down to search from the position of the insertion point to the end of the selection or document, Up to search from the position of the insertion point to the beginning of the selection or document, or All to search the entire document beginning at the insertion point.

4. Choose any of the options described below to limit the search results.

5. Select Find Next to start the search. The first instance of the document item you are searching for appears highlighted. To edit the document, click in the document window or press **Alt+F6** to activate the document window. Click in the Find dialog box when you are finished with your edit.

6. If necessary, select Find Next to find the next instance of the document item.

7. When Word reaches the beginning or end of the document during the search process, a dialog box appears asking if you want to continue the search. Select Yes to continue the search back to the location of the insertion point.

8. Choose OK to remove the message box that appears to tell you when the search is complete.

9. When you are done, select Cancel or press **Esc**.

To repeat your last search after you have closed the Find dialog box, press **Shift+F4** to search without opening the dialog box.

You can also choose Replace in the Find dialog box. The searching options you selected appear in the Replace dialog box. See *To Replace Document Items*, below.

To Replace Document Items

1. Select Edit ➤ Replace (**Ctrl+H**), or choose Replace in the Find dialog box. The Replace dialog box appears.

2. Type the search text in the Find What text box, or select Find What and highlight one of the items in the list. The last four items you have searched for appear in the list.

3. Type the replacement text in the Replace With text box.

4. Select Search, then choose Down to search from the position of the insertion point to the end of the selection or document, Up to search from the position of the insertion point to the beginning of the selection or document, or All to search the entire document beginning at the insertion point.

5. Choose any of the options described below to limit the search results.

6. Select Find Next to start the search. The first instance of the search item appears highlighted.

7. Select Replace to replace the item, or choose Find Next to find the next instance without replacing this instance.

8. Repeat steps 6 and 7 as necessary.

9. When Word reaches the beginning or end of the document during the search process, a dialog box appears asking if you want to continue the search. Select Yes to continue the search back to the location of the insertion point.

10. Choose OK to remove the message box that tells you when the search is complete.

11. When you have finished replacing, choose Cancel or press **Esc** to return to your document.

Select Replace All to automatically replace all instances of the search item

OPTIONS   The following options are available in both the Find and the Replace dialog boxes:

Match Case   Finds the document items with the exact uppercase and lowercase letters. If Small Caps or All Caps formatting was applied, the case is ignored.

Find <u>W</u>hole Words Only	Finds only text that is a whole word. In a search for formatting, only whole words with the specified formatting applied are found.
Use Pattern <u>M</u>atching	Uses the advanced search criteria shown in Table II.3.
Sounds <u>L</u>ike	Finds homophones of the text in the Fi<u>n</u>d What text box.
No Forma<u>t</u>ting	Removes all specified formatting from the search.
F<u>o</u>rmat	Displays a pop-up list of formatting options. Choose <u>F</u>ont, <u>P</u>aragraph, <u>L</u>anguage, or <u>S</u>tyle to display each command's dialog box. Choose the search formatting in each dialog box. You can search for formatting only, without searching for any text.
Sp<u>e</u>cial	Displays a pop-up list of special characters. Choose a character in the list to enter in the Fi<u>n</u>d What text box.

NOTES To edit your document while the Replace dialog box is displayed, click in the document window or press **Alt+F6** to activate it. Click in the Replace dialog box when you are finished with your edit.

To delete the search item, remove all the characters from the Replace With text box.

To find text without searching for formatting, make sure no formats appear in the area under the Fi<u>n</u>d What text box. To find text with formatting, enter the text in the Fi<u>n</u>d What text box, then choose F<u>o</u>rmat and select the format for which you want to search. To find formatting only, remove all the characters from the Fi<u>n</u>d What text box and make sure the insertion point is in the text box. Then choose F<u>o</u>rmat and select the format for which you want to search. When the search criteria is correct, select <u>F</u>ind Next and perform your search or replace operation.

 **See Also** *Font; Go To; Language; Paragraphs; Styles*

Use Format ➤ Font to apply a format to selected characters or the next characters you type. You can apply a different font and size, or other text attributes such as bold or italic formatting.

To Apply Fonts to Characters

Use drop-down lists and buttons on the Formatting toolbar (displayed by default) to change the Font or Font Size, and to apply Bold, Italic, or Underline format. Or use shortcut keys to bypass many of the options in the Font dialog box or to remove formatting from selected text. Table II.4 shows the character formatting shortcut keys.

Table II.4: The character-formatting shortcut keys

Press These Keys	To Apply This Format
Ctrl+B	Bold
Ctrl+I	Italic
Ctrl+U	Underline
Ctrl+Shift+W	Word underline
Ctrl+Shift+D	Double underline
Ctrl+=	Subscript
Ctrl+Shift+=	Superscript
Ctrl+Shift+K	Small caps
Ctrl+Shift+A	All caps

Table II.4: The character-formatting shortcut keys (continued)

Press These Keys	To Apply This Format
Shift+F3	(Cycle through Convert Case options)
Ctrl+Shift+H	Hidden text
Ctrl+Shift+C	Copy formats
Ctrl+Shift+V	Paste formats
Ctrl+Spacebar	Remove formats
Ctrl+Shift+F, ↓	Select Font box on Formatting toolbar
Ctrl+Shift+Q	Symbol font on Formatting toolbar
Ctrl+Shift+P, ↓	Point size on Formatting toolbar

1. Move the insertion point to where you want to begin new formatting, or select the text you want to format.

2. If necessary, choose Format ➤ Font. The Font dialog box appears. Select either the Font tab or the Character Spacing tab.

3. Choose any of the options (described below) on each tab.

4. Choose OK in the Font dialog box.

 OPTIONS   The Font tab options are as follows:

Font	Type the name of the font in the text box, or select the name in the Font list box.
Font Style	Type the style to apply to the font, or select Regular (the default for each font), Bold, Italic, or Bold Italic in the list. Not all of the style options are available for every font.
Size	Type the size for the font in the Size text box or select a size from the list box.

Underline	Choose one of the attributes in the drop-down list.
Color	Choose one of the 16 colors available in the drop-down list. The text will display in color on a color monitor, and print in color on a color printer.
Effects	Strikethrough draws a line through text that does not have a revision line through it. Superscript raises the text above the base line, and Subscript lowers the text below the baseline. Hidden hides the text in the document. It will not appear on your screen or in a printed document. Small Caps displays all the text in reduced-size capital letters, and All Caps displays the text in regular-size capital letters.

The options on the Character Spacing tab are as follows:

Spacing	In the drop-down list, select Normal to use the default spacing for the font, Condensed to decrease the spacing between characters, or Expanded to increase the spacing. Change the measurement in the By text box for Condensed or Expanded.
Position	Choose Normal in the drop-down list to place characters on the baseline. Choose Raised or Lowered to adjust the text up or down three points. Enter a number between 0 and 63 in the By text box to raise or lower the text by a different measurement. To include fractional points as the measurement, enter the fraction as a decimal.

Kerning for Fonts	Changes the spacing between characters automatically. Enter the font size that Word uses as the base in the Points and Above text box. Larger text is kerned automatically. Kerning can only be used with TrueType or ATM fonts, and only with fonts above a certain size.
Default	Choose the button and select Yes to change the default fonts and attributes in the document template to the options selected on either tab.

To Copy Formats to Characters

You can use the new Format Painter feature to copy the formats of selected text to other text.

1. Select the text whose formatting you want to copy.

2. Click on the **Format Painter** button to copy a format to only one selection, or double-click to copy the format to multiple selections. The Format Painter pointer appears as an I beam with a paintbrush when you move the mouse pointer into the document window.

3. Select the text to which you want to copy the format. As you highlight the text, the format is copied to it.

4. Repeat step 3 for each set of characters to which you want to copy the format.

5. If necessary, click the **Format Painter** button or press **Esc** to turn off the feature.

You can also use the formatting shortcut keys to copy a selected format, then paste it to other text. If you copy a paragraph mark, you can paste the paragraph style and any additional formats applied to the paragraph to other text. If you select some paragraph text and the paragraph mark to copy, the paragraph style and any additional formats applied to the first character selected can be pasted to other text.

 **See Also** *Repeat*

FOOTNOTES AND ENDNOTES

Use footnotes and endnotes to provide explanations or references to marked items in the text of a document. Footnotes appear at the bottom of the page where the marked item appears, separated from document text by a horizontal line. Endnotes appear at the end of the chapter, section, or document, separated by a horizontal line. However, you can change the location of either to suit your needs. Your documents can contain both footnotes and endnotes.

Word automatically updates footnote and endnote numbering when you add or delete a marked item in your document, and places the text of either in the correct position in your document. Because Word manages footnotes and endnotes the same way, they will be called "notes" in this entry.

To Add a Note

By default, footnotes are numbered 1, 2, 3, etc., and endnotes are numbered i, ii, iii, etc. You can change the note number format.

1. Select View ➤ Normal or click the **Normal View** button on the horizontal scroll bar to make sure you are in Normal view.

2. Move the insertion point to where you want to add a note reference mark and select Insert ➤ Footnote. The Footnote and Endnote dialog box appears.

3. Select either Footnote or Endnote in the Insert area of the dialog box.

4. In the Numbering area, select either AutoNumber to automatically update the note numbers in your document, or

Custom Mark to use a symbol to mark the reference in
your document. If you select Custom Mark, choose Symbol and select the symbol you want to use, then select OK
in the Symbol dialog box.

5.   If necessary, select Options to change the format of the
notes in your document. See *Options* below for a description of the available options.

6.   Choose OK in the Footnote and Endnote dialog box. The
note pane appears at the bottom of your screen.

7.   Type the note text in the note pane. If necessary, click in
the document window to keep the note pane open and
continue editing your document. Press **Alt+Ctrl+F** to add
another footnote to the document or **Alt+Ctrl+E** to another endnote to the document at the location of the insertion point. Click in the note pane to edit the note.

8.   When you are finished adding notes to the document or
editing notes in the note pane, click Close (**Alt+Shift+C**)
in the note pane.

OPTIONS   When you choose Options in the Footnotes
and Endnotes dialog box, the Note Options dialog box appears with
the All Footnotes and All Endnotes tabs.

Place At	Select the drop-down list. For footnotes, choose Bottom of Page to print the note just above the bottom margin on the same page as its reference mark, or Beneath Text to print the note just below the last line of text on the page. For endnotes, choose End of Section to print notes just after the last line of the section its reference mark is in, or End of Document to print notes after the last line of the document text.
Number Format	Select the drop-down list, then choose Arabic numbers, lowercase or uppercase letters or Roman numerals, or symbols in the list as the numbering format for notes.

Start At   Type or adjust the number at which you
               want to start the note numbering.

Numbering   For footnotes or endnotes, choose
               Continuous to number the notes throughout
               the document in sequence, or Restart Each
               Section to start note numbers in each section
               with the number in the Start At text box. For
               Footnotes, a third option is to Restart Each
               Page, which starts numbering on each page
               with the number in the Start At text box.

Convert   Choose Convert All Footnotes To Endnotes,
               Convert All Endnotes to Footnotes, or Swap
               Footnotes and Endnotes to convert both
               simultaneously, then choose OK in the
               Convert Notes dialog box. You can convert a
               single footnote or endnote in the note pane
               or the actual note. Move the insertion point
               into the text of the note and click the right
               mouse button. Select the Convert to
               Footnote or Convert to Endnote command.

To Display Notes

Display notes in your document in either the Normal or Page Layout view. The note text appears in the note pane in Normal view,
and in its correct location in Page Layout view. There are several
ways to display the text of notes.

- Double-click on the note mark in your document. In Normal view, the note pane opens and the insertion point
  moves to the note's text in the pane. In Page Layout view,
  the insertion point moves to the note's text.

- Choose View ➤ Footnotes. In Normal view, the note pane
  opens to the last viewed note type. You can change the
  view of the note type by selecting All Footnotes or All Endnotes in the drop-down list at the top of the note pane. In
  Page Layout view, the View Footnotes dialog box appears.
  Choose View Footnote Area or View Endnote Area, then

choose OK. The insertion point moves to the note text area in the document.

Double-click on the note mark in the note pane or note area of your document to move back to the mark in the document text. Alternately, click the right mouse button on the note mark and select Go To Endnote or Go To Footnote to move the insertion point to the document window.

To Edit Notes

Notes have two parts—the note mark and the note text. To copy, delete, or move a note, select the note reference mark in your document. You can edit the text of a note directly.

Use one of the following methods to move a note :

- Drag the note reference mark to a new location.

- Select the note reference mark, then select Edit ➤ Cut (**Ctrl+X**) or click the **Cut** button on the Standard toolbar. Alternately, right-click on the selected note mark and choose Cut from the shortcut menu. Move the insertion point to the new note location in your document and select Edit ➤ Paste (**Ctrl+V**), or click the **Paste** button on the Standard toolbar. Alternatively, move the insertion point to where you want to move the note and right-click, then choose Paste from the shortcut menu.

To copy a note in your document:

- Hold down **Ctrl** while you drag the note reference mark to a different location.

- Select the note reference mark, then select Edit ➤ Copy (**Ctrl+C**), click the **Copy** button on the Standard toolbar, or click the right mouse button and choose Copy. Move the insertion point to the different note location in your document and select Edit ➤ Paste (**Ctrl+V**), click the **Paste** button on the Standard toolbar, or click the right mouse button and select Paste from the shortcut menu.

Use one of the following methods to delete notes in your document:

- Select the note reference mark in your document, then press **Backspace** or **Del**.

- Choose Edit ➤ Replace (**Ctrl+H**), and then select Special. Select Footnote Mark or Endnote mark in the pop-up list, delete the contents of the Replace With text box, and select Replace All.

To Edit Note Separators

By default, a short horizontal line, called a *note separator,* separates notes from the document text. If the notes on one page continue on the next, a longer line, called a *continuation separator,* separates the notes from the document text. You can edit these separators so that informational text appears above them.

1. If necessary, select View ➤ Normal or click the **Normal View** button on the horizontal scroll bar.

2. Select All Footnotes or All Endnotes in the drop-down list at the top of the note pane, and choose the note pane whose separator you want to edit.

3. Select the drop-down list at the top of the note pane, and select Footnote Separator or Endnote Separator, which appears as a two-inch line, or Footnote Continuation Separator or Endnote Continuation Separator, which appears as a line spanning from the left to the right margin.

4. Select the separator and press **Backspace** or **Del** to delete it. Or type the text you want above the note separator.

5. To return the separator to its default appearance, select Reset. When you are finished editing the note pane, select Close (**Alt+Shift+C**) to close the pane.

NOTES   You can edit the format of the text of individual notes, or you can change the style of the note text to edit the format of all the footnotes or endnotes. To make the note style available to all documents you create based on the current template, add the style to the template.

Add cross-references to note references to refer several notes to one source.

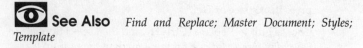 **See Also**   *Find and Replace; Master Document; Styles; Template*

Word comes with many built-in forms already created for you. However, you can easily create custom forms in Word by adding form-field codes to a document template. You can create on-line forms or design forms to be printed and filled out by hand. Create a new document template for each custom form.

To Create a Form

1. Select File ➤ New to display the New dialog box, then select Template and choose OK to create a new template.

2. Type the text of the form.

3. Move the insertion point to where you want the form's user to enter or choose data. Then select Insert ➤ Form Field to display the Form Field dialog box or click the right mouse button on a displayed toolbar and select Forms from the shortcut menu to display the Forms toolbar.

4. Select one of the option buttons in the Type area of the dialog box to define the type of form field you want to insert. You can select a Text, Check Box, or Drop-Down form field. Or click on the **Text Form Field** button, **Check Box Form Field** button, or the **Drop-Down Form Field** button on the Forms toolbar.

5. Choose Options, then select the options you want to add to the form field and choose OK. Or, click on the **Form Field Options** button on the Forms toolbar. The options available for each type of form field are described below.

6. Repeat steps 3–5 as necessary to complete your form.

7. Select Tools ➤ Protect Document, select Forms, then choose OK; or click on the **Protect Form** button on the Forms toolbar.

8. Save the form as a template.

9. Select File ➤ Close to close the template.

If you did not display the Forms toolbar in step 3 above, you can choose Show Toolbar in the Form Field dialog box to display it.

 OPTIONS

Type   In the Text Form Field Options dialog box, highlight the type of text form field you want at the insertion point in the drop-down list. Choose Regular Text to make the user type characters such as text, numbers, symbols, or spaces. Choose Number to make the user type a number in the form field, or Date for a form field requiring a date. Highlight the Current Date/Current Time option to make Word enter the system date or time. Select Calculation to have Word perform a calculation in the form field.

Default Text   Type the default text to display in a text form field. If the form field type is Calculation, the text box is called Expression instead of Default Text.

Check Box Size	In the Check Box Form Field Options dialog box, select <u>A</u>uto to size the check box relative to the font and point size of the surrounding text or select the <u>E</u>xactly option button, then enter the measurement.
Move	Change the order of the <u>I</u>tems in Drop-Down List using the ↑ or ↓ buttons.
<u>M</u>aximum Length	Choose Unlimited to define an inexact length for the form field contents. You can also type or adjust a number between 1 and 255 in the text box.
Text <u>F</u>ormat	In the drop-down list, choose Uppercase, Lowercase, First Capital, or Title Case as the text format. If Calculation is the type of form field, the text box is called Number Format. Select general, decimal, comma, currency, percent, or percent with two decimal places as the number format.
Default Value	Select Not Chec<u>k</u>ed to clear the check box in a check box form field by default. Select <u>C</u>hecked to select the check box in the form field by default.
<u>D</u>rop-Down Item	Type the text you want as an item in a drop-down list.
<u>A</u>dd	Adds the selected <u>D</u>rop-Down Item to the <u>I</u>tems in Drop-Down List.
<u>R</u>emove	Removes the selected <u>D</u>rop-Down Item from the <u>I</u>tems in Drop-Down List.
<u>I</u>tems in Drop-Down List	Highlight the item to <u>A</u>dd or <u>R</u>emove.
Run Macro On	Choose the corresponding drop-down list, then select a macro from the Entr<u>y</u> list to run when the user enters the form field, and/or from the E<u>x</u>it list to run when the user leaves the form field.

Field Settings   Type the Bookmark name in the text box
                  that will be associated with the form field
                  and referenced by a macro. For a text-box
                  form field, select the Fill-In Enabled check
                  box to allow the form field to be filled in
                  online. For a check-box form field, select
                  the Check Box Enabled check box to allow
                  the form field to be filled in online. For a
                  drop-down form field, select the Drop-
                  Down Enabled check box to allow the form
                  field to be filled in online. Clear the check
                  box to make the form field read-only.

Add Help Text   See the Add Help Text options right below.

The following options are available in the Form Field Help Text
dialog box when you choose the Add Help Text button in any of
the form-field type Options dialog boxes. These options appear on
both the Status Bar tab and the Help Key (F1) tab:

None   Makes no help available for the form field.

AutoText   In the drop-down list, choose the AutoText
Entry   entry attached to the template that you
                  want to use as the help text.

Type Your   Type the form field's help text in the text box.
Own

To Fill In a Form Online

Once you have assigned document protection to a form, you can
easily move the insertion point from one form field to the next to
fill in an online form.

1.   Select File ➤ New to make the New dialog box appear.

2.   Highlight the name of the template that contains the form
         you want to fill in. Make sure Document is selected in the
         New area, then choose OK.

3.   Use any of the methods described in Table II.5 below to
         move from one form field to another. Fill in the form as
         necessary.

Table II.5: Methods used to move from one form field to another

Key Sequence	Action
Tab, ↵, or ↓	Enter data and move to next field
Shift+Tab or ↑	Move to previous field
F4 or Alt+↓	Select drop-down list in field
↑ or ↓	Select drop-down–list item
Spacebar or X	Select a check box in field, or clear a selected check box
F1	Display field Help
Ctrl+Tab	Insert a tab in a field

4. Save the filled-in form as a file.

To Protect a Form

The form fields will not be activated until you protect the document. If you protect the document while you are creating the template, the protection is saved with the template. Any documents you open based on the template will also be protected. If you need to edit a form field, select Tools ➤ Unprotect Document or click on the **Protect Form** button on the Forms toolbar to remove the document protection.

When you protect a form, Word makes several things happen to it:

- You can only move to, select, or type in form fields or unprotected sections of the document.

- The form fields are activated according to the type of form chosen for each field. Macros assigned to a field as you enter or exit and the help you have assigned to a form field are also activated.

• Results of the fields are displayed rather than the field codes.

• Some of the document commands are not available at all. Other commands are available only for the form fields and unprotected sections of the form.

• Users who know the password for the document protection can unprotect the document.

To protect a form, select Tools ➤ Protect Document.

NOTES You can apply formatting to a text form field in your document with Format ➤ Font or the buttons on the Formatting toolbar.

Use tables, frames, borders, and shading to create an attractive, useful online form. To print only the form field data to fill in a preprinted form, select the Print Data Only for Forms check box on the Print tab in the Options dialog box. To save only the form field data, select the Save Data Only for Forms check box on the Save tab in the Options dialog box.

See Also *Borders and Shading; Document; Document Protection; Field Codes; Frames; Print; Save/Save As; Tables; Template; Toolbars*

FRAMES

Use a frame to position text or graphics on a page in your document. Frames will expand to accommodate their contents, and text will wrap around a frame in the document. You can also resize a frame to meet your needs.

If you are in Page Layout or Print Preview view, you can easily see how the frame and its contents look in your document, and use the mouse to resize or reposition a frame.

To Add a Frame

1. With nothing selected, choose Insert ➤ Frame. Alternately, click on the **Drawing** button on the Standard toolbar to display the Drawing toolbar, and click on the **Insert Frame** button. The mouse pointer changes into a crosshair.

2. Move the crosshair to the top-left corner of where you want to insert the frame. Drag the pointer down and to the right. A dotted rectangle appears as you insert and size the frame.

3. Release the mouse button to insert the frame.

You can also add a frame around items already in your document.

1. Select the text or graphic.

2. Choose Insert ➤ Frame, or click the **Insert Frame** button on the Drawing toolbar. A selected frame appears around the item.

To Edit or Format a Frame

You can use your mouse to edit the frame, or you can format the frame to the exact specifications you want to use in a document

1. Select the frame.

2. Select Format ➤ Frame to specify the exact size and place-ment of the frame. The options in the Frame dialog box are described below. Alternatively, use your mouse to resize or reposition the frame.

3. Choose OK in the Frame dialog box.

 **OPTIONS**

Text Wrapping	Choose None in the Text Wrapping area to break the document text above the frame and make text continue below the frame. Choose Around to make text flow around the frame. There must be at least one inch between the margin or column boundary and the frame for the text to wrap completely around the frame.

Size	Select the Width drop-down list, then choose Auto to allow a frame to span from the left margin to the right margin; or choose Exactly, then enter an exact width for the frame in the At text box. Choose the Height drop-down list, then choose Auto to allow the frame to be as tall as the height of its tallest contents. Alternatively, choose At Least to specify the minimum height for the frame or Exactly to specify the exact height for the frame in the At text box.
Horizontal	Type an exact measurement or select the Position drop-down list to specify the frame's position on the page, relative to the location specified in the Relative To drop-down list. Choose Left, Right, Center, Inside, and Outside as the position relative to a margin, the edge of the page, or in a column. Enter how much space will separate the frame horizontally from surrounding text in the Distance from Text text box.
Vertical	Type an exact measurement or select the Position drop-down list to specify the frame's position on the page, relative to the location specified in the Relative To drop-down list. You can choose Top, Bottom, or Center as the position relative to a margin, the top of the page, or in a column. Enter how much space will separate the frame from surrounding text in the Distance from Text text box. Select Move with Text to move the frame vertically on the page as you add or delete paragraphs in the document. Select Lock Anchor to anchor the frame to a specific paragraph.
Remove Frame	Removes the frame. The frame's contents are moved to the paragraph above the one where the frame was anchored.

To remove the frame and delete its contents, select the frame and press **Backspace** or **Del**.

To Select a Frame

To edit or move a frame and its contents, first select the frame. A selected frame appears with eight small black squares, called *handles*, on its crosshatched borders. If you place the insertion point inside the frame, only the crosshatched border of the frame appears.

The mouse pointer changes shape according to what function it can perform. If the pointer is placed along the frame's border, it appears as a positioning pointer with a four-headed arrow. You can drag the frame to any position on the page. If the pointer is placed inside the frame, it appears as an I beam, and you can edit or select the contents of the frame. When you place the pointer on one of a selected frame's handles, a two-headed sizing pointer appears. Drag the handle outward to make the frame larger, or inward to make the frame smaller.

To select a frame, point to its border. When the mouse pointer appears as a positioning pointer, click to select the frame.

NOTES   Type and format text in a frame just like text in a document. However, if you are applying styles to your text, apply the style before you add a frame to the text. Otherwise, the style may reposition the frame. Use the indent markers on the Ruler or Format ➤ Paragraph to indent a paragraph within a frame. Point to the frame and click the right mouse button if you want to choose one of the commands on the shortcut menu to format the contents of the frame.

Include a caption with the item in the frame so that if the item moves, the caption moves with it. You can insert captions with Insert ➤ Caption or by typing the text inside the frame.

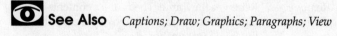 **See Also**   *Captions; Draw; Graphics; Paragraphs; View*

GO TO

To move quickly to another document location, use <u>E</u>dit ➤ <u>G</u>o To (**F5**) to go to a specific document item.

To Go to a Document Location

1. Choose <u>E</u>dit ➤ <u>G</u>o To (**F5**). The Go To dialog box appears.

2. Highlight a document item in the Go To <u>W</u>hat list box.

3. To go to the next specified document item, choose Nex<u>t</u>; to go to the previous item, choose <u>P</u>revious. You can also type a positive or negative number in the <u>E</u>nter *document item* text box, then choose Go <u>T</u>o to move the insertion point forwards or backwards through the document to that item.

4. Select Close in the Go To dialog box.

You can also type **s*n*p*n,*** where *n* is the number, in the Enter *document item* text box to move to a specific section number and page number in that section.

 NOTES   Use **Shift+F5** to move to the last three positions of the insertion point. You can also display the Go To dialog box by double-clicking the left half of the Status Bar.

⊚ See Also   *Document; Find and Replace*

GRAMMAR

Use Word's Grammar feature to check your document text for grammatical or stylistic errors, and to simultaneously check for spelling errors. You control the rules Grammar uses to check for text errors by setting options on the Grammar tab in the Options dialog box. The grammar check begins where the insertion point is.

To Check Grammar

1. Press **Ctrl+Home** to move the insertion point to the beginning of the document, or select the text you want to check.

2. Choose <u>T</u>ools ➤ <u>G</u>rammar.

3. Choose the appropriate option in the dialog box. The options are described below.

4. When you have finished checking your document text, select OK in the Readability Statistics message box to return to your document.

 **OPTIONS**

<u>S</u>entence	The text box displays a sentence whose grammar is questioned. You can accept the change Grammar suggests, edit the sentence in the text box, or not change the sentence at all.
Suggestions	The suggested changes to the displayed sentence appear in the list box. Select the change to implement.
<u>E</u>xplain	Provides Grammar's explanation of why the selected sentence is incorrect. Double-click on the message box's control icon to close the message box.
<u>O</u>ptions	Displays the Grammar tab of the Options dialog box where you can choose the rules Grammar uses to check your document text. See *To Set Grammar Check Options* below.
Undo <u>L</u>ast	Reverses the last change made in the <u>S</u>entence text box.

Ignore	Skips making any of the suggested changes to the item in question, and marks the next text in question.
Next Sentence	Skips errors in the current sentence and moves to the next sentence with errors.
Change	Accepts the highlighted item in the Suggestions list box or accepts the edits you performed to the text in the Sentence text box.
Ignore Rule	Skips making any corrections to the text in the Sentence text box, and ignores any questions about similar items during the grammar check.

 **See Also**   *Spelling; Thesaurus*

GRAPHICS

Enhance the appearance of your documents by adding graphics to them. There are several ways you can add a graphic to a document—paste the graphic from the Clipboard, draw a graphic using the Drawing tools, or use Insert ➤ Picture to insert a picture in your document. See *Cut, Copy, and Paste* for information on pasting a graphic into your document. See *Draw* for information on adding a graphic with the Drawing tools.

To Edit a Graphic

Once you have imported a graphic into a document, you can apply borders and shading to it, resize it, or crop parts of the graphic from the original. You can also add a frame to a graphic in your document. Use a frame when you want to move the graphic or add shading around it. When a graphic is selected, eight handles appear around it.

- To add a border, select the graphic, then click on the **Borders** button on the Formatting toolbar, or choose Format ➤ Borders and Shading.

- To add shading around a graphic, select the graphic, then select Insert ➤ Frame. Use the options in the Frame dialog box to resize the frame so it is larger than the graphic, then select the Shading drop-down list on the Borders toolbar or Format ➤ Borders and Shading, and apply the shading you want to the area between the frame and the graphic.

- To resize a graphic, select the graphic, then move the pointer to one of its handles. When the pointer appears as a two-headed arrow, drag a corner handle to resize the graphic but keep its original proportions, or drag one of its middle handles to resize the graphic but lose its original proportions.

- To crop a graphic, select the graphic, then press **Shift** while dragging a handle towards the center of the graphic. The cropping measurements are displayed in the Status bar. Or use Format ➤ Picture to crop the picture to your exact specifications, then select OK in the Picture dialog box. See *Options* below for a descriptions of the options in the Picture dialog box.

- To edit a graphic extensively, double-click on it. The graphic appears in a separate window, and the Drawing toolbar is displayed above the Status bar. Use the Drawing tools to add, remove, apply color or line styles, or add text to the graphic.

 **OPTIONS**

Crop From	Enter the measurement to crop from the Left, Right, Top, or Bottom of the graphic.
Scaling	Type or adjust the percentage of the graphic's original Width and Height.
Size	Type or adjust the measurement for the graphic's Width and Height.

Original Size	Displays the original size of the graphic.
Reset	Return the graphic to its original size and cropping.
Frame	Display the Frame dialog box. You must use options in the dialog box to format the frame around a graphic.

To Import a Graphic

To insert a graphic that is saved in a file on disk, use Insert ➤ Picture to place the graphic in your document. Word can interpret many different graphics file formats, including those created in other applications.

Word also comes with many clip-art files you can use in your documents. They can be found in the WINWORD6\CLIPART directory, and are in .WMF (Windows Metafile) format.

1. Move the insertion point to where you want the graphic to appear.

2. Choose Insert ➤ Picture. The Insert Picture dialog box appears.

3. Select the name of the file you want to import in the File Name list box.

4. Select Preview Picture to see a sample of the graphic.

5. If necessary, select the Save Picture in Document check box to save Word's interpretation of a graphic rather than the actual graphic in your document.

6. Select OK in the dialog box to insert the picture in your document.

To Save a Graphic in Native Format

If you import a graphic created on a different platform, for example, a graphic created on a Macintosh, Word saves both the original graphic and its interpretation of the graphic in your document. You can save disk space by saving the graphic only in Word's interpretation, its native format, in your document.

1. Select Tools ➤ Options, and choose the Save tab.
2. Select Save Native Picture Formats Only .
3. Choose OK in the Options dialog box.

NOTES To change the application window used to extensively edit a graphic you have imported, choose Tools ➤ Options and select the Edit tab. In the Picture Editor drop-down list, choose Microsoft Word or Microsoft Drawing.

See Also *Chart; Cut, Copy, and Paste; Draw; Frames*

HEADERS AND FOOTERS

Headers are text or graphics displayed and printed in the top margin of each page of your document. Footers are text or graphics displayed and printed in the bottom margin of each page of your document.

You can easily add headers and footers to a document with View ➤ Header and Footer. The command displays the Header and Footer toolbar, which you use to create or edit a header or footer in your document, changes the display to Page Layout view, and moves the insertion point to the header area on the current page.

To Create or Edit a Header and Footer

1. Select View ➤ Header and Footer. The Header and Footer toolbar appears and the header area of the current page is activated.

2. Type the text you want for the header of your document. Use Word's regular formatting techniques to format your text.

3. Click on the **Switch Between Header and Footer** button on the Header and Footer toolbar to activate the footer.

4. Type the text and apply the formatting you want for the footer.

5. Click on the corresponding button on the Header and Footer toolbar to insert the current **Date**, the current **Time**, or the **Page Numbers** field codes. Click on the **Switch Between Header and Footer** button as necessary.

6. To change any of the page-layout options for your document, click on the **Page Setup** button to display the Page Setup dialog box.

7. To adjust the distance between the header or footer and the text of the document, drag the margin boundary on the vertical ruler up or down.

8. Optionally, click on the **Show/Hide Document Text** button to display or hide the regular text in your document.

9. When you have finished creating or editing your header and footer, click the **Close** button on the Header and Footer toolbar to return to your document.

To Display Headers and Footers

To edit or update a field code in a header or footer, activate the header or footer and display the Header and Footer toolbar.

- If you are in Page Layout view, you can edit a header or footer by double-clicking on either the header or footer. The header is activated, and the Header and Footer toolbar appears.

- If you are in Normal view, select View ➤ Header and Footer.

To Make the First Page Header and Footer Different

1. Select View ➤ Header and Footer. The Header and Footer toolbar appears, and the header is activated.

2. Click on the **Page Setup** button on the Header and Footer toolbar. Select the Layout tab in the Page Setup dialog box.

3. Select Different First Page in the Headers and Footers area, then select OK in the Page Setup dialog box.

4. If necessary, create the header and footer for the first page. To omit a header and footer on the first page, leave the areas blank.

5. Click on the **Show Next** button to move to the next header area, then create the header and footer for the rest of the document. Click on the **Switch Between Header and Footer** button as necessary.

6. Click the **Close** button on the Header and Footer toolbar to return to your document.

To Make Odd and Even Page Headers and Footers Different

1. Select View ➤ Header and Footer. The Header and Footer toolbar appears, and the header is activated.

2. Click on the **Page Setup** button on the Header and Footer toolbar. Select the Layout tab in the Page Setup dialog box.

3. Select Different Odd and Even in the Headers and Footers area, then select OK in the Page Setup dialog box.

4. If necessary, click the **Show Previous** or **Show Next** button on the Header and Footer toolbar to move to an even page number. Create the header and footer for even pages. Click the **Switch Between Header and Footer** button as necessary.

5. Click the **Show Previous** or **Show Next** button on the Header and Footer toolbar to move to an odd page number, then create the header and footer for odd pages. Click the **Switch Between Header and Footer** button as necessary.

6. Click the **Close** button on the Header and Footer toolbar to return to your document.

To Make Headers and Footers Sectional

If you create headers and footers in documents that contain more than one section, all the headers and footers will be the same for the entire document. The sections are connected so that the contents of the headers and footers are the same, and *Same as Previous* appears in the top right corner of the header or footer area.

To create different headers and footers for a section, disconnect the previous section's header and footer. All subsequent sections will then have the same header and footer as the section after the broken connection, unless you break the connection for those sections as well.

1. Move the insertion point into the section where you want different headers and footers.

2. Choose <u>V</u>iew ➤ <u>H</u>eader and Footer.

3. Click on the **Same As Previous** button on the Header and footer toolbar to break the connection to the previous section.

4. Select the header and footer, and press Backspace or **Del** to delete the text. Click the **Switch Between Header and Footer** button as necessary.

5. Create the new header and footer. Click the **Switch Between Header and Footer** button as necessary.

6. If necessary, move the insertion point into the next section and repeat steps 3–5 to create different headers and footers for that section.

7. To reestablish the connection with the previous section, move the insertion point into a section with a broken connection and click the **Same As Previous** button on the Header and Footer toolbar.

8. Click the **Close** button on the Header and Footer toolbar to return to your document.

NOTES   Use a negative indent to print a header or footer in the left or right margin.

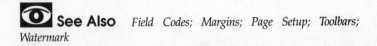 **See Also**   *Field   Codes;   Margins;   Page   Setup;   Toolbars;* *Watermark*

N E W

HELP

Word for Windows contains extensive online help. You can search for keywords, view demonstrations with Examples and Demos, display WordBasic commands, or read step-by-step instructions for a task. You can get Help by using commands on the Help menu or by double-clicking on the Help button on the Standard toolbar.

To Access Context-Sensitive Help

There are several ways you can quickly get help about the current command or dialog box.

- Double-click on the **Help** button on the Standard toolbar to display the Search dialog box, then begin typing the key word or topic on which you want help.

- Press **F1** when a menu command is highlighted.

- Select the Help button in a dialog box.

- Click on one of the underlined topics in a Help window.

In addition, you can use the menu commands in the Help window to add a bookmark or a note to a topic, to copy a help topic to the Clipboard, or to print a help topic.

- Select Bookmark ➤ Define to place a bookmark in a help topic. The names of bookmarks you have defined appear on the Bookmark drop-down menu. Select the bookmark you want to go to.

- Select Edit ➤ Copy to copy the text of a Help topic to the Clipboard. You can paste it into a document and edit or print the text.

- Select Edit ➤ Annotate to add a note to a Help topic. Topics with annotations appear with a paper clip beside the topic title. Click on the paper clip to display the Annotate window with your note.

- Choose File ➤ Print Topic to print the current Help topic.

To Use How-To Help

Often when you select a Help topic, a How To window will open on your screen. You can use the buttons on the window's button bar to control How To Help. Select **Print** to print the topic, **Index** to display the Help Index, **On Top** to make the How To window stay on top of your document so you can refer to it, or Close to close the How To window.

NOTES　Use the Examples and Demos topic for a demonstration of a Word for Windows procedure. Click on the button beside the procedure you want to see.

See Also　*Tip of the Day*

HIDDEN TEXT

To hide text in your document, select the text and format it as hidden text. By default, hidden text will not appear on your screen or be printed. However, if you display hidden text, it will appear on the screen with a dotted underline and will print as regular document text. You can also choose to print hidden text without first displaying it.

To Create Hidden Text

1. Select the text you want to hide.

2. Choose Format ➤ Font, and then choose the Font tab.

3. Select Hidden in the Effects area of the dialog box.

4. Choose OK in the Font dialog box to hide the selected text.

You can also press **Ctrl+Shift+H** to hide selected text.

To Display Hidden Text

To display all nonprinting characters, click the **Show/Hide ¶** button on the Standard toolbar.

To display only hidden text without displaying other nonprinting characters, choose Tools ➤ Options and select the View tab. Clear any selected check boxes in the Nonprinting Characters area of the tab except for the Hidden Text check box. Select OK in the Options dialog box.

To Print Hidden Text

When you print hidden text, your document may not print as it appears on your screen. Display the hidden text you want to print before you print your document so that you can adjust page and line breaks if necessary.

1. Choose File ➤ Print to display the Print dialog box, then choose Options. Or choose Tools ➤ Options and select the Print tab.

2. Select the Hidden Text check box in the Include with Document area of the dialog box.

3. Choose OK in the Options dialog box. If necessary, choose OK again in the Print dialog box.

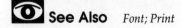 **See Also** *Font; Print*

HYPHENATION

By default, Word wraps text to the next line in your document. Use hyphenation to control the ragged appearance of left-aligned text or the amount of white space on a line of justified text. Hyphenation can also be used to improve the appearance of text in columns. You can hyphenate text utomatically or manually.

To Automatically Hyphenate Words

1. Select Tools ➤ Hyphenation. The Hyphenation dialog box appears.

2. Select the Automatically Hyphenate Document check box to turn on automatic hyphenation.

3. Select the Hyphenate Words in CAPS check box to allow hyphenation in words in uppercase letters.

4. Enter the measurement in the Hyphenation Zone text box. The measurement indicates the greatest amount of white space allowed beside the margin. Word hyphenates words that fall in the zone.

5. Type or adjust the number in the Limit Consecutive Hyphen To text box. The number indicates how many consecutive lines of text can be hyphenated.

6. Choose OK in the Hyphenation dialog box.

The larger the hyphenation zone, the fewer the number of hyphens. The smaller the hyphenation zone, the greater the number of hyphens, but the text along the right margin is less ragged.

To Exclude Automatic Hyphenation from Paragraphs

All paragraph formatting and information is contained in the paragraph mark.

1. Select the paragraphs that have automatic hyphenation.

2. Choose Format ➤ Paragraph, and select the Text Flow tab.

3. Select the Don't Hyphenate check box.

4. Select OK in the Paragraph dialog box.

To Manually Hyphenate Words

To hyphenate part of a document or choose which words will be hyphenated, choose Manual in the Hyphenation dialog box to accept or reject each word that would be hyphenated in your document. Wait until you have added all text and document items to your document before you manually hyphenate it.

1. Select Tools ➤ Hyphenation, then select Manual in the Hyphenation dialog box. The Manual Hyphenation dialog box appears, and the first hyphenated word in the document appears in the Hyphenate At text box.

2. If necessary, click at the position where you want the hyphen to appear in the word to change the suggested hyphenation. Then select Yes to hyphenate the word, or No to skip hyphenation in the word. To eliminate hyphenation in the rest of the document, select Cancel or press **Esc.**

3. When all the hyphenated words have been reviewed in the document, a message box appears to tell you that hyphenation is finished. Select OK.

You can also directly insert a *nonbreaking* hyphen or an *optional* hyphen in your document. Nonbreaking hyphens are used in words that should not break at the end of a line, such as "father-in-law", or "built-in". Optional hyphens are used to break the word at the end of a line.

• Press **Ctrl+Hyphen** to insert an optional hyphen at the position of the insertion point.

• Press **Ctrl+Shift+Hyphen** to insert a nonbreaking hyphen at the position of the insertion point.

👁 See Also *Paragraphs*

INDENT

An indent is the distance between the text and the margins in your document. You can change the indent for an entire paragraph or for the paragraph's first line, and you can indent text from either the left or the right margin.

To Indent One Paragraph

To indent a single paragraph to the next or previous tab stop, move the insertion point into the paragraph or select the paragraph, then use one of the following methods:

- To increase the indentation of an entire paragraph to the next tab stop, click on the **Increase Indent** button on the Formatting toolbar or press **Ctrl+M**.

- To decrease the indentation of an entire paragraph to the previous tab stop, click on the **Decrease Indent** button on the Formatting toolbar or press **Ctrl+Shift+M**.

- To create a hanging indent, press **Ctrl+T**.

- To decrease a hanging indent, press **Ctrl+Shift+T**.

To Indent a Paragraph with Exact Measurements

1. Select Format ➤ Paragraph, and then select the Indents and Spacing tab in the Paragraph dialog box.

2. In the Indentation area, enter the distance in the appropriate text box that you want to indent the paragraph from the Left or Right margin. Enter a negative number in the corresponding text box if you want text to appear in either margin.

3. Select the Special drop-down list to define the indents you want for the first line of the paragraph. You can choose None, First Line, or Hanging.

4. Enter the distance the first line will be indented in the By text box.

5. Choose OK in the Paragraph dialog box.

To Use the Ruler

Use the indent markers on the Ruler to quickly change the indentation of the paragraph the insertion point is in. Figure II.1 shows the Ruler and the indentation markers.

- Drag the first-line indent marker on the Ruler the distance you want to indent the first line from the left margin.

- Drag the left indent marker to indent all of the paragraph except the first line the distance specified on the Ruler from the left margin. This creates a hanging indent.

- Drag the right indent marker to indent all lines of the paragraph the distance specified on the Ruler from the right margin.

NOTES Use one of the above methods to indent your text rather than pressing the Tab key or the Spacebar, which may not align your text properly.

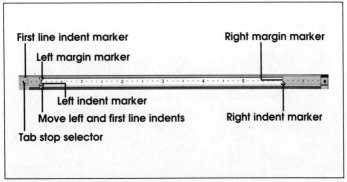

Figure II.1: The Ruler and indentation markers

⊙ See Also *Margins; Paragraphs; Ruler; Tabs; Unit of Measurement*

INDEX

To create an index for a document, first mark the index entries, then compile the index. Index entries can be marked in the main document text and in footnotes and endnotes. You can also create cross-references to other entries, or show a topic covered within a range of pages.

To Automatically Mark Index Entries

Once you have created a concordance file, you can automatically mark the index entries in your document. Only the first entry in a paragraph is marked.

1. Open the document that will contain the index and select Insert ➤ Index and Tables. Choose the Index tab in the Index and Tables dialog box.

2. Select AutoMark to display the Open Index AutoMark dialog box.

3. Type or select the name of the concordance file you want to use in the File Name list box.

4. Choose OK in the Open Index AutoMark dialog box.

To Create a Concordance File

One way to mark index entries is to create a *concordance file,* which you can use to automatically mark index entries in your document. A concordance file is a separate document that contains two columns of information—the words and phrases you want to index in your document, and the actual index entries you want to generate. Text in a concordance file is case sensitive.

1. Select File ➤ New and choose OK, or press **Ctrl+N** or click the **New** button on the Standard toolbar.

2. Select Table ➤ Insert Table, then choose OK in the Insert Table dialog box to insert a two-column table in the document.

3. In the first column, enter the text (exactly as it appears in your document) that you want to mark as an index entry in your document.

4. Enter the index entry for the item in the first column, exactly as it will appear in the index, in the second column.

5. Repeat steps 3 and 4 as necessary.

6. Save the concordance file.

To Create Index Entries

You can mark your index entries in the document that will contain the index. An XE (index entry) field is inserted as hidden text at a marked entry. The field code displays no results in your document, but the field results are displayed in the index when it is compiled.

1. Select the text you want to mark in your document or move the insertion point to where you want to insert an entry. Then press **Alt+Shift+X** to open the Mark Index Entry dialog box.

2. If necessary, edit the text you selected in the Main Entry text box, or type the entry you want to insert in your document in the text box.

3. Type the subentry text in the Subentry text box. To create a subentry for the subentry, type a colon after the subentry in the Subentry text box, then type the sub-subentry.

4. Select Bold and or Italic to format the entry's page number.

5. Select Mark to mark the entry, or select Mark All to mark the exact text for each occurrence of the entry in your document.

6. Repeat steps 1–5 as necessary.

7. Choose Close in the Mark Index Entry dialog box.

You can format the text of an entry and any subentries by selecting the text in the Main Entry or Subentry text boxes. Apply formatting to the selection with the appropriate formatting shortcut keys.

Only the first occurrence of the entry text in a paragraph is marked.

To Edit Index Entries

Word inserts the XE (index entry) field code for each index entry you mark in your document. To edit a marked entry, click the **Show/Hide ¶** button on the Standard toolbar to display all non-printing characters.

You can use switches with the XE field code to define how the entry will appear. For example, you can format the entry's page number in bold or italic, redefine the type of entry, include a range of pages in the entry, or enter text instead of page numbers in the entry. Double-click on the **Help** button on the Standard toolbar, then type XE and press ↵ twice to display online help for the XE field code.

- To edit the text of the index entry, select the characters between the " ".

- Select the entire field code, including the field-code characters { }, then press **Backspace** or **Del** to delete the entry.

You can also edit the text of an index you have inserted in your document. However, if you edit the marked entries in your document text, you will lose all the edits when you update the index.

To Insert an Index in a Document

You can insert the index in a predefined or customized format in your document and choose a format for the subentry text.

1. After you have marked all your index entries in the document, move the insertion point to where you want the index.

2. Type and format any text you want to appear before the generated index.

3. Choose Insert ➤ Index and Tables. Select the Index tab.

4. Select any of the options described below.

5.   Choose OK in the Index and Tables dialog box to insert the Index field code in your document.

When you insert an index in a document, you are actually inserting the Index field code. You can see the field code if you move the insertion point into the index and click the right mouse button. Select Toggle Field Codes to display the Index code. Right-click on the Index code and select Toggle Field Codes again to display the results of the Index code.

 **OPTIONS**

Type	Select Indented to indent subentries on lines below the main index entry, or select Run-in to place subentries on the same line as the main entry.
Formats	Highlight one of the predefined formats in the list box, or select Custom Style and change any of the predefined formats.
Right Align Page Numbers	Aligns the main entry and subentry page numbers along the right margin. If you selected Run-in as the type of index, the check box is not available.
Columns	Enter the number of columns you want in the index. Choose Auto to keep the same number of columns in the format you choose, or select 1–4 columns. Columns do not appear in the Preview area of the dialog box.
Tab Leader	Select the tab leader you want to place before page numbers in the index from the drop-down list.
Modify	If you choose Custom Style as the format for the index, select Modify to modify the Index styles that appear in the dialog box.

To Show a Cross-Reference in an Entry

1. In the Mark Index Entry dialog box, enter the text for the entry in the Main Entry text box, then type any necessary subentry text in the Subentry text box.

2. Select Cross-reference. The insertion point moves into the text box after "See ". Type the text for the cross-reference.

3. Select Mark.

4. Repeat steps 1–3 as necessary.

5. Choose Close in the Mark Index Entry dialog box.

You can edit all the text in the Cross-reference text box and apply formatting to selected text in the text box with the appropriate shortcut keys.

To Show a Range of Pages in an Entry

1. In the Mark Index Entry dialog box, enter the text for the entry in the Main Entry text box, then type any necessary subentry text in the Subentry text box.

2. Select Page Range.

3. Type a name in the Bookmark text box for the page range and select Mark.

4. Select the text you want the page range entry to reference, then choose Edit ➤ Bookmark.

5. Enter the same bookmark name for the selection as the name you typed in the Bookmark text box of the Mark Index Entry dialog box.

6. Choose Add in the Bookmark dialog box.

7. Mark additional index entries as necessary in the Mark Index Entry dialog box.

To Update the Index

If you edit your document after you have inserted the index or mark any new entries, update the index to make sure it is correct.

- Move the insertion point into the index and click the right mouse button. Select Update Field to update the index.

- Move the insertion point into the index and press **F9** (Update) to update the Index field code.

NOTES   Chapter numbers included with page numbers and inserted using the Insert ➤ Page Numbers command are included in the index.

You can also mark index entries with Insert ➤ Index and Tables. Select the Index tab, and choose Mark Entry to mark index entries.

See Also   *Alignment; Columns; Field Codes; Hidden Text; Styles; Table of Authorities; Table of Contents; Tabs*

INSERT FILE

You can insert a file or part of a file, even one created with another application, into a Word document. You can also link the file to the document, so if the original file is changed, you can update the changes in your document.

To Insert a File

1. Move the insertion point to where you want to insert the file, then select Insert ➤ File. The File dialog box appears.

2. Select the name of the file you want to insert in the File Name list box, or choose Network to display the Network-

Drive Connection dialog box to connect to a network drive.

3. If necessary, select List Files of Type and choose the type of file in the File Name list box.

4. To insert only a part of the selected file into your document, type the range, range name, or bookmark name in the Range text box.

5. Select Confirm Conversion to approve the converter Word uses to convert a file created in a different application.

6. Select the Link to File check box to establish a link between the document and the file you are inserting.

7. Choose OK in the File dialog box to insert the selected file.

You can choose Find File to open the Find File dialog box and search for the file you want to insert.

INSERT/OVERTYPE

When you first start Word, it is in Insert mode. By default, characters you enter into a document are inserted into the text—they push existing characters to the right. If you want, you can change the typing mode to Overtype. Then characters you type will replace existing characters located at the insertion point.

To Change to Overtype Mode

You can use the mouse or the keyboard to switch from Insert to Overtype mode:

- Double-click on OVR on the status bar.
- Press the **Insert** key.

When you are in Overtype mode, OVR on the Status bar appears in black letters. When you are in Insert mode, OVR appears grayed on the Status bar. Use either method to switch back to Insert mode.

To Set Insert/Overtype Defaults

1. Select Tools ➤ Options, then select the Edit tab.

2. Select Use the INS Key for Paste to have the Insert key paste the contents of the Clipboard at the insertion point.

3. Select Overtype Mode to change to Overtype mode.

4. Choose OK in the Options dialog box.

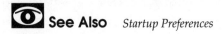 **See Also** *Startup Preferences*

KEEP TEXT TOGETHER

Word adjusts the pagination of your document according to the absence or presence of several different document items. For example, page breaks are affected by hyphenation, displaying hidden text, footnotes, and graphics. Graphics cannot be broken—each must appear as a single whole item. If a graphic will not fit on a page, Word adjusts the page break to occur before the graphic. However, you can keep some specified text together on a page.

To Keep Text Together on a Page

1. Move the insertion point to the paragraph whose text you want to control.

2. Select Format ➤ Paragraph, then choose the Text Flow tab.

3. Select or clear the appropriate check box in the Pagination area of the dialog box to control the document's page breaks. The check box options are described below.

4. Choose OK in the Paragraph dialog box.

 **OPTIONS**

Widow/Or- Stops a single line from appearing on the
phan Control first line at the top or on the last line at the
 bottom of a page, or a single word from
 appearing as the last line of a paragraph.
 Widow/orphan control applies to the
 entire document.

Keep Lines Stops a page break from occurring within a
Together paragraph.

Keep with Keeps two or more paragraphs together on
Next the same page. Move the insertion point
 into the first paragraph of two you want to
 keep together, or select each paragraph
 except the last one that you want to keep
 together, then follow the steps above.

Page Break Places the page break before the paragraph.
Before

NOTES Remove any manual page breaks you have placed in text you want to keep together.

A small black square appears next to paragraphs for which you have selected Keep Lines Together, Keep with Next, or Page Break Before in Normal view mode, but it will not appear on the printed document.

See Also *Footnotes and Endnotes; Graphics; Hidden Text; Hyphenation; Page Break; Paragraphs; Repagination*

KEYBOARD

Change the assignment of shortcut keys in Word to those that are easy for you to remember and use, or assign shortcut keys to a command, macro, font, style, AutoText entry, or a special symbol. Save the changed key assignments to a template so they will be available whenever you create or edit a document based on that template.

To Change Shortcut Key Assignments

1. Choose Tools ➤ Customize and choose the Keyboard tab.

2. Highlight the template in which to store the new key assignments in the Save Changes In drop-down list.

3. Select the kind of command or item you want to change the key assignment of in the Categories list box.

4. Highlight the name of the command or item you want to assign shortcut keys to in the *Item Name* list box to the right of the Categories list box. The item's current shortcut key assignment appears in the Current Keys list box.

5. Move the insertion point into the Press New Shortcut Key text box, then press the shortcut keys you want to assign to the item. If the key sequence is already assigned to another command or item, the Currently Assigned To message appears below the text box.

6. To assign the shortcut key sequence, select Assign.

7. Repeat steps 2–6 as necessary for additional shortcut keys.

8. Choose Close in the Customize dialog box.

To Delete a Shortcut Key

1. Choose Tools ➤ Customize and choose the Keyboard tab.

2. Select the template that contains the shortcut key in the Save Changes In drop-down list.

3. Select the kind of command or item that contains the shortcut key you want to delete in the Categories list box. Then select the item whose shortcut key you want to remove in the *Item Name* list box.

4. Highlight the shortcut key sequence you want to delete in the Current Keys list box, then choose Remove.

5. Repeat steps 2–4 as necessary.

6. Choose Close in the Customize dialog box.

NOTES   To return all the changed key assignments to their original Word key assignments, select Reset All on the Keyboard tab in the Customize dialog box.

You can also display the Keyboard tab of the Customize dialog box with only one selected command displayed. Press **Alt+Ctrl++** (plus sign on the numeric keypad), then move the mouse pointer, which has changed into a command sign (⌘), to select a command from the menu bar.

See Also   *Menus; Toolbar*

Word allows you to print one label or a page of labels with the same text. Select one of Word's built-in label definitions (based on many different Avery® label types and sizes) or customize a label definition.

Before you select a type of label, select and set up the printer on which you want to print the labels. The printer driver selected determines how the labels will be set up and printed.

To Print a Label

1. If necessary, select the text in your document you want to print. Choose Tools ➤ Envelopes and Labels and select the Labels tab. Selected text appears in the Address text box.

2. If necessary, type the text you want to appear on the label in the Address text box.

3. Click on the Label area of the dialog box or select Options to display the Label Options dialog box. Define the label and printer specifications and choose OK. The dialog box options are described below.

4. In the Print area of the Labels tab, select Full Page of the Same Label to print the text in the Address text box on each label or select Single Label to print the text on only one label. Then enter the Row and Column numbers describing the location of the label on the sheet of labels.

5. Select Print.

OPTIONS   The remaining options on the Labels tab are as follows:

Use Return Address	Prints a return address on a single label or on each label on the page. If you type a new return address and select Print or New Document, Word asks if you want to make it the default return address for all future documents created with the same template. Choose Yes or No.
Delivery Point Bar Code	Includes the POSTNET bar code on a mailing label.
Label	A sample of the options selected appears in the Label area. Click on the sample to display the Label Options dialog box.
New Document	Places a full sheet of labels in a table in a new document so you can save the document as a file.

Select the necessary options in the Label Options dialog box, then select OK. The options are as follows:

Printer Information	Select Dot Matrix or Laser in the Printer Information area. If you have selected Laser as the type of printer, select the Tray drop-down list, then highlight how the labels will be fed to the printer.
Label Products	Highlight the kind of label you are using in the drop-down list.
Product Number	Highlight the label you want to use in the list box.
Label Information	A description of the highlighted label in the Product Number list box appears here.
Details	Displays the *Label Type* Information dialog box for customizing the selected label.

Select the necessary options in the Label *Type* Information dialog box, then select OK. The options are as follows:

Top Margin	Enter the distance between the top edge of the page and the top edge of the labels in the first row for a page of laser printer labels. The top margin for dot matrix labels should be 0.
Side Margin	Enter the distance between the left edge of the page and the left edge of the labels in the first column.
Vertical Pitch	Enter the distance between the top edge of one label and the top edge of the label below.
Horizontal Pitch	Enter the distance between the left edge of one label and the left edge of the label on its right.
Label Height	Enter the distance between the top and bottom edges of a label.

Label <u>W</u>idth   Enter the distance between the left and right edges of a label.

Number <u>A</u>cross   Enter a number describing the number of labels in a row on the page.

Number <u>D</u>own   Enter a number describing the number of labels in a column on the page.

NOTES   You can also use Mail Merge to print labels if you have created a data file.

See Also   *Envelopes; Mail Merge; Print; Save/Save As*

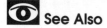

LANGUAGE

You can change the language or omit proofing for a document or for selected text in a document. If you change the language, you must have the dictionary of the language or a related language to check the spelling.

The dictionary that comes with Word for Windows is an English language dictionary, containing both American English and British English spellings for words. To check the British spelling of the text in a document, change the language to English (UK).

To Change the Language Used to Check Spelling

1. Select the text to proof in a different language or not to proof at all.

2. Choose <u>T</u>ools ➤ <u>L</u>anguage.

3. In the <u>M</u>ark Selected Text As list box, highlight the name of the language you want to use to proof the selection, or highlight the (no proofing) entry to prevent the selection from being proofed.

4. To use the language you selected as the default for all documents created with the same template, choose De-fault, then select Yes.

5. Choose OK in the Language dialog box.

 **NOTES** If you often create documents in a different lan-guage, create a style for that language that contains the language format. Then apply the style to text you want to proof in Word.

See Also *Spelling; Styles*

LINE NUMBERING

You can add line numbers to documents when you need to refer to individual lines in the text. The text in tables, footnotes, endnotes, headers, footers, and frames is not line numbered. Line numbers appear on screen if you are in Page Layout or Print Preview mode, and are printed with the document.

To Add Line Numbering

1. Move the insertion point to where you want line number-ing to begin in your document. If the document contains more than one section, choose Edit ➤ Select All to add line numbering to the entire document.

2. Choose File ➤ Page Setup, then choose the Layout tab.

3. Select Line Numbers.

4. Select the Add Line Numbering check box.

5. Choose any of the options described below, then select OK in the Line Numbers dialog box.

6. Choose OK in the Page Setup dialog box.

 **OPTIONS**

Start At   Enter the starting line number.

From Text   Enter the distance from the right edge of numbers to the left edge of the line of text.

Count By   Enter the increments used in line numbering. All lines in the document are counted, but numbers appear only for the lines specified in the Count By text box.

Numbering   Choose Restart Each Page to begin with line 1 at the top of each page, Restart Each Section to begin with line 1 at the beginning of each document section, or Continuous to specify consecutive numbers throughout the document.

To remove line numbers, clear the Add Line Numbering check box in the Line Numbers dialog box.

To Suppress Line Numbering

You can also remove numbers from selected paragraphs in a document. The numbering will resume for text after the selection.

1. Select the paragraphs whose line numbers you want to remove.

2. Choose Format ➤ Paragraph, and select the Text Flow tab.

3. Select the Suppress Line Numbers check box.

4. Choose OK in the Paragraph dialog box.

NOTES   Change the line number format by modifying the line numbering style.

Line numbers are printed in the margins or between columns of text unless the margin or space between columns is not wide enough. View the document in Print Preview mode before you print it to make sure the line numbers will print.

 **See Also**   *Columns; Margins; Paragraphs; Styles; View*

LINE SPACING

A paragraph's line spacing defines the height of each line in the text. The height of a line depends on the font used in the paragraph. If, for example, you select a 12-point font, the height of a single-spaced line would be just over 12 points, so some white space, called *leading*, could be included above the text and below the baseline of the text above. The height of a 12-point double-spaced line would be about 24 points. You can set the line spacing to adjust the amount of white space that appears above the text in each line.

If a line contains an oversized character, its line spacing is adjusted to accommodate the character. You can adjust the line spacing so that all the lines are evenly spaced in the paragraph.

By default, line spacing in Word is set for single spacing. You can set the line spacing to a preset definition or customize the line spacing for your document.

To Change the Line Spacing in a Paragraph

You can change the line spacing of the paragraph that contains the insertion point, or of selected paragraphs with shortcut keys.

- Press **Ctrl+1** to reset the selection to single-spaced lines.

- Press **Ctrl+5** to set the selection to 1.5 line spacing.

- Press **Ctrl+2** to set the selection to double-spaced lines.

To Set the Line Spacing Options

1. Move the insertion point into the paragraph or select the paragraphs whose spacing you want to change.

2. Choose Format ➤ Paragraph and choose the Indents and Spacing tab.

3. Select one of the line spacing options (described below) in the Line Spacing drop-down list in the Spacing area.

4. Choose OK in the Paragraph dialog box.

 **OPTIONS**

- Select Single to adjust the line height to the tallest character in the line. Single spacing varies depending on font size.

- Select 1.5 Lines to adjust the line height to 1.5 times that of single spacing.

- Select Double to double the line height of single spacing.

- Choose At Least to define the minimum line height. Word can adjust the line spacing for various types of characters.

- Choose Exactly to define an exact line height in the At text box that Word cannot adjust.

- Select Multiple to adjust the line spacing to a specific multiple of single spaced text, then specify the number of lines in the At text box. The default number of lines is 3.

- Enter the amount of spacing you want in each line in the At text box. Word will not adjust the spacing you define.

 **See Also** *Dropped Capital; Line*

LINKS

You can link two Word documents, or link a document created with another application to a Word document. When documents are linked, the data in the source document can be changed, then automatically updated in the destination (Word) document. Links in Word documents are stored as field codes.

To Create a Link

The source document must be saved before you can link data in it to your Word document.

1. With the source file open, select the data you want to link to your Word document.

2. Select Edit ➤ Copy (**Ctrl+C**) in the source file.

3. Activate the Word document, and move the insertion point to where you want to link the source data.

4. Select Edit ➤ Paste Special. The Paste Special dialog box appears with the path and file name of the selected data in the Source area of the dialog box.

5. Choose Paste Link to insert the selected data into the Word document as a link.

6. In the As list box, choose how to paste the information in your Word document. The options are described below.

7. Select the Display as Icon check box if you want the link to appear as an icon in your Word document.

8. Optionally, you can change the icon in your document by selecting Change Icon, selecting the necessary options in the Change Icon dialog box, then choosing OK. See *Options* below for additional information.

9. Choose OK in the Paste Special dialog box.

🔆 **OPTIONS**   The other option in the Paste Special dialog box is <u>P</u>aste. Select this if you want to paste the selection into your Word document in one of the formats listed below.

The type of link options in the <u>A</u>s list box are as follows:

Application Name Object	The Clipboard contents are linked to the document as a graphic.
Formatted Text (RTF)	The Clipboard contents are linked to the document as text data with its current formatting.
Unformatted Text	The contents of the Clipboard are linked to the document as unformatted text.
Picture	The Clipboard contents, such as those from a .WMF file, are linked to the document as a graphic.
Bitmap	The contents of the Clipboard, such as those from a .BMP file, are linked to the document as a bitmap.

The options in the Change Icon dialog box are as follows:

<u>I</u>con	Choose an icon in the list box to appear in the Word destination document.
<u>C</u>aption	If necessary, type the text you want to appear under the icon in your document.
<u>B</u>rowse	Select the button to search for other files that may contain additional icons from which you can choose.
File Name	The name of the file that contains the icons displayed in the <u>I</u>con list box appears in the File Name area of the dialog box.

To Create a Link from Within Word for Windows

You can insert a link to all the data in a file into your document without leaving Word:

1.   Move the insertion point to where you want the link.

2. Choose Insert ➤ Object and select the Create from File tab.

3. In the File Name list box, select the name of the file you want to link to the Word document. Choose Find File to display the Find File dialog box or Network to display the Disk Connect dialog box when you need to search for the file you want to link.

4. Select the Link to File check box to link the data in the source to the destination Word document.

5. Select the Display as Icon check box if you want the link to appear as an icon in your Word document.

6. Optionally, select Change Icon to change the icon to display in your document, then select OK. The Change Icon dialog box options are described above.

7. Select OK in the Object dialog box.

To Edit a Link

You can break an established link, reconnect a link to a file that has been moved or renamed, store the link as a picture in your document, specify how the link will be updated, update the link yourself, or lock a link in your document.

1. With the Word document that contains the link active, choose Edit ➤ Links. The Links dialog box appears.

2. Choose any of the options, described below, to edit a link.

3. Choose the OK button in the Links dialog box.

 OPTIONS

Source File   The list box displays the names and source files of all the links in the active document. Highlight the link to modify, then perform the necessary edits. You can select more than one link in the list box by holding down **Ctrl** as you click on additional links.

Item   Displays the name or range of the link.

Type   Displays the name of the source application.

Update   Displays the update option you have selected for the link. Choose <u>A</u>utomatic for the link to be updated whenever the source is changed. Choose <u>M</u>anual to update a selected link in the Source File list box by selecting <u>U</u>pdate Now in the Links dialog box or selecting the link in your document and pressing the **F9** (Update) key to update the link.

<u>U</u>pdate Now   Updates all the links highlighted in the <u>S</u>ource File list box.

<u>O</u>pen Source   To edit the data in the linked item, choose this button to open the source document of the link highlighted in the <u>S</u>ource File list box. You can also select the linked item in your document, then choose <u>E</u>dit ➤ Linked *Application* <u>O</u>bject to open the source document of the selected link.

Cha<u>n</u>ge Source   Highlight the link or links you lost when the source was moved or renamed in the <u>S</u>ource File list box. Then choose the button to display the Change Source dialog box. Select the name of the file to link in the File <u>N</u>ame list box. The name or range of the item that is linked appears in the <u>I</u>tem text box. You can type a different name or range for the link. Choose OK in the Change Source dialog box when you have selected the new file name containing the link. If your document contains other links to the original source, a message box asks you to confirm the new source for the other links. Choose <u>Y</u>es to change the source file.

Break Link	Breaks the link highlighted in the Source File list box. Or select the link in your document and press **Ctrl+Shift+F9** to break it. The current data remains in your Word document, but can no longer be updated or reconnected.
Locked	Stops a selected link from being updated (alternatively, select the link in your document and press **Ctrl+F11** to lock the link). Clear the Locked check box or press **Ctrl+Shift+F11** when you want to update the link.
Save Picture in Document	Saves the link as a picture of the linked data in your document rather than the actual information. Clear the check box if the link is a graphic and you want to reduce the size of your Word document. However, the link will take longer to display because Word must interpret the data in the source file and then create the picture.

NOTES You can have Word update manual links to your document each time you print. Select Tools ➤ Options, then choose the Print tab. Select the Update Links check box in the Printing Options area of the dialog box, then choose OK.

Changes you make to the formatting of the item in the source are not updated if the *MERGEFORMAT switch is in the field.

Highlight the links in your Word destination document so you will not edit them. All the edits will be lost when you update the links. Choose Tools ➤ Options and select the View tab. In the Show area, highlight Always in the Field Shading drop-down list. Then select OK in the Options dialog box.

You can also highlight the source of the links in a Word source document. Choose Tools ➤ Options and select the View tab. Select the Bookmarks check box in the Show area, then select OK. The source data appears on your screen with gray brackets.

See Also   *Field Codes; Find File; Object Linking and Embedding; Open; Print*

You can record uncomplicated macros to automate tasks that you regularly perform. Macros can be assigned to menus, shortcut keys, or toolbars for easy access. With the new Macro toolbar, you can edit a macro you have recorded or written.

Word comes with many useful global macros already built-in. The macros are stored in the MACRO.DOT template. You can assign these macros to a toolbar, menu, or key combination, or you can run them with Tools ➤ Macro.

To Delete a Macro

1.   Choose Tools ➤ Macro to display the Macro dialog box.

2.   Select the name of the macro you want to delete in the Macro Name list box.

3.   Choose Delete, then choose Yes.

4.   Select Close to return to your document.

To Edit a Macro

Word compiles macros you record in its WordBasic programming language. To edit a macro you have recorded (or written using WordBasic), open the macro in the macro editing window.

1.   Choose Tools ➤ Macro. The Macro dialog box appears.

2. Select the macro to edit in the Macro Name list box.

3. Select Edit. The macro appears in a document window below the Macro toolbar.

4. Choose the appropriate buttons to perform your edits (or type them in).

5. Select File ➤ Save Template or click on the **Save** button on the Standard toolbar to save the macro to its current name. To rename the macro, choose File ➤ Save Copy As, and type a name in the File Name text box. Then choose OK in the Save As dialog box.

To Record a Macro

Record the commands and keystrokes you use to perform a task you often repeat while working in Word. While you are recording, the Macro Record toolbar appears on your screen, and the mouse pointer appears with a graphic of a cassette tape. You can use the mouse to select commands or to scroll while you are recording a macro, but not to select text or move the insertion point.

If you accidentally record something you didn't want to record in your macro, immediately select Edit ➤ Undo or click on the **Undo** button on the Standard toolbar. The action you reversed will not play back when you run the macro.

1. Select Tools ➤ Macro, then choose Record in the Macro dialog box. Alternatively, double-click on **REC** on the Status bar.

2. Type a name for the macro in the Record Macro Name text box, and a description in the Description text box.

3. In the Assign Macro To area of the Record Macro dialog box, select Toolbars, Menus, or Keyboard as the method of access to the macro. See the corresponding entry for an explanation of the available options for each.

4.   If necessary, select the Make Macro Available To drop-down list and select All documents (NORMAL.DOT) or the active template.

5.   Choose OK in the Record Macro dialog box.

6.   Select the commands and type the keystrokes necessary for the macro.

7.   Double-click on **REC** on the Status bar or click the **Stop** button on the Macro Record toolbar to stop recording the macro. Or select Tools ➤ Macro and select Stop Recording, then choose Close in the Macro dialog box.

To temporarily stop recording the commands and keystrokes in a macro, click on the **Pause** button on the Macro Record toolbar. Click on it again to resume recording.

To Run a Macro

You can easily run a macro that you have assigned to a toolbar, menu, or shortcut key sequence by clicking on the toolbar button, selecting the menu command, or pressing the key combination. You can also run a macro using Tools ➤ Macro.

1.   Choose Tools ➤ Macro. The Macro dialog box appears.

2.   Select the macro in the Macro Name list box.

3.   Choose the Run button.

NOTES   You can also use WordBasic to create more complex macros in Word, including instructions that cannot be recorded.

For information on renaming a macro, moving or copying a macro to a different template, or deleting a macro that is in a different template, see *To Use Organizer* in the Template entry.

See Also   *AutoCorrect; AutoText; Keyboard; Menus; Status Bar; Template; Toolbars*

MAIL

If you have a compatible mail application such as Microsoft Mail, you can send an online document to other people for their comments, revisions, or to fill in a form. You can choose how the document is sent—to each person simultaneously, or to selected people in a specific order.

To Mail an Online Document

1. With the document you want to send online active, choose File ➤ Add Routing Slip. Your name appears in the From area of the Routing Slip dialog box.

2. To select the people to whom you want to send the document, choose Address. Highlight the name of a person in the To list box and choose Add. When you have selected the name of each recipient, select OK.

3. If necessary, use the ↑ and ↓ Move buttons to arrange the names in the list in the order for the document to be routed.

4. Type the subject of the document in the Subject text box.

5. Type any messages or instructions to the document's recipients in the Message Text text box.

6. Select the routing method in the Route to Recipients area of the dialog box. Choose One After Another to send the document to the people in the order they are listed in the To list box, or choose All at Once to simultaneously send a copy of the document to all the people in the To list box.

7. Select the Return When Done check box to have the document returned after it is reviewed and each person selects the File ➤ Send command.

8. If you sent the document to each person in the order they are listed in the To list box, select the Track Status check box to receive a message when the document is forwarded to the next person on the list.

9. Choose Revisions, Annotations, or Forms from the Protect For drop-down list to protect the document from any changes to its text.

10. Select Route to send the document.

To return to your document and edit it before you send it, choose Add Slip. Then select File ➤ Send and choose Yes.

To Merge Revisions

If you send the document simultaneously to the people on the list, each person's revisions or annotations will be sent back to you in a separate document. You can merge the revisions or annotations into the original document, where up to eight individuals' revisions will appear in different colors.

1. With the revised document active, select Tools ➤ Revisions. The Revisions dialog box appears.

2. Select Merge Revisions.

3. Select the name of the original document file in the Original File Name list box.

4. Choose OK in the Merge Revisions dialog box.

Alternatively, double-click on the document's icon in your returned mail message to open the revised document. If you select Yes when asked if you want to merge the revisions, the Merge Revisions dialog box appears with the original document filename already selected. Select OK to merge the document.

NOTES A document sent to each person in the order they appear in the list collects all the revisions and annotations in one document.

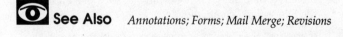 **See Also** *Annotations; Forms; Mail Merge; Revisions*

NEW
MAIL MERGE

Use Word's Mail Merge feature to combine a *data source* with a *main document*. The data source is a Word database file that contains the information that changes for each document. The main document contains the text that stays the same in each document and merge field codes that instruct Word where to insert the data source information.

To perform a Mail Merge, first, specify the main document; second, specify the data source; and third, perform the merge.

To Create a Main Document

1. Open a new or existing document.

2. Select Tools ➤ Mail Merge. The Mail Merge Helper dialog box appears.

3. Choose Create in the Main Document area.

4. Select the type of document to create, then select Active Window to confirm that you want your main document to be the current document. The Mail Merge toolbar appears above the main document window. See *Options* below for a description of the types of documents you can create.

 OPTIONS

Form Letters	Sets up the main document for a form letter.
Mailing Labels	Creates a main document for mailing labels.
Envelopes	Sets up a main document for envelopes.

Catalog	Organizes lists of data.
Restore to Normal Word Document	Changes a main document back into a normal Word document by removing the relationship it has with the data source.

To Designate a Data Source

Second, open or create a new data file as the data source for the main document.

1. Select Get Data in the Data Source area of the Mail Merge Helper dialog box.

2. Choose one of the options in the drop-down list. The options are described below.

 **OPTIONS**

Create Data Source	The Create Data Source dialog box appears. Type a new field name in the Field Name text box. A field name must begin with a letter and can contain up to 40 characters including letters, numbers, and the underline character, but no spaces. Select Add Field Name to add the new field name to the list. Highlight a name in the Field Names in Header Row list box that you want to move or delete, then select the ↑ or ↓ Move button to change the position of the highlighted field name, or choose Remove Field Name to remove the name from the list box. Select MS Query to search the database for records that match criteria with the Microsoft Query program. When you have finished creating the data source, select OK in the Create Data Source dialog box, then save the data source file. Select Edit Data Source to display the Data Form dialog box, or Edit Main Document to return to the main document.

Open Data Source	Displays the Open Data Source dialog box. Select the file in the File Name list box that contains the data you want to open. Select Confirm Conversion to approve the converter Word uses to convert a file created in a different application. Then choose OK.
Header Options	Choose this option to create or open a header source document, a document that contains only the merge fields of a data source. When you save a header source file, you can use the merge fields it contains in many different merge documents. If you must change a merge field, you can change it in the header document instead of in each of your data source documents. When you select Header Options, a dialog box appears asking you to Create or Open a header document. The Create Header Source and Open Header Source dialog boxes are similar to the Create Data Source and the Open Data Source dialog boxes.

To Edit a Data File

1. Choose Edit Data Source after you have saved a newly created data source, or click the **Edit Data Source** button on the Mail Merge toolbar.

2. Type the appropriate information in the first text box and press ↵ to enter that information in the record.

3. Press **Tab** to move the insertion point to the next text box, then enter the appropriate information.

4. Repeat step 3 until all the fields for the first record are completed. Then select Add New to add data to the first record.

5. Repeat steps 2–4 until all the records for the data source have been added. Then choose OK in the Data Form dialog box.

6. Save the data source file.

💡 **OPTIONS**   Other options in the Data Form dialog box are as follows:

Record	Type the number of the record you want to display. Alternately, click on **First Record**, **Previous Record**, **Next Record**, or **Last Record** in the Record area.
Delete	Remove the displayed record from the data source.
Restore	Undo the changes made to the displayed record.
Find	Display the Find in Field dialog box to quickly locate text in a selected data field. Type the characters to find in the Find What text box. Choose the field name to search for the text in the In Field drop-down list. Then choose Find First or Find Next to find the first occurrence or the next occurrence. Each time Word finds the specified text, the record found is displayed in the Data Form dialog box. Choose Close when you have completed your search.
View Source	Display all the records in the data source in a table format. Each record is a row in the table, and the Database toolbar appears above the document window.

To Edit the Main Document

After you have specified an open data source, you can insert the field names in the data source document as merge fields in the main document.

1. Edit the text and other document items in the main document window.

2. Move the insertion point to where you want to add a merge field, then click on the **Insert Merge Field** button on the Mail Merge toolbar and choose the field. Type any characters or punctuation to include with the field.

3. Repeat step 2 for each merge field in your main document.

4. Save the main document.

To Insert or Edit Fields in the Data Source

1. Choose the **Edit Data Source** button on the Mail Merge toolbar in the main document window.

2. Choose View Source.

3. Click on the **Manage Fields** button on the Database toolbar. The Manage Fields dialog box appears.

4. Type a new name in the Field Name text box.

5. Select Add to add the new field to the existing fields.

6. Optionally, highlight a field in the Field Names in Header Row list box, then select Remove to remove the field name from the data source.

7. Optionally, highlight a field name in the Field Names in Header Row list box, then select Rename. Type the new name in the New Field Name text box, then choose OK in the Rename Field dialog box.

8. Choose OK in the Manage Fields dialog box.

You can add the new field information directly in the data source document window, or you can choose the **Data Form** button on the Database toolbar, then add the new field data into each record.

To Merge the Data File and the Main Document

1. In the main document window, click the **View Merged Data** button on the Mail Merge toolbar. The fields from the first data record are displayed in the main document merge-field locations.

2. Optionally, select or type another record number in the Go To Record text box on the Mail Merge toolbar.

3. On the Mail Merge toolbar, click **Merge to Printer** to print all the merged documents, **Merge to New Document** to send all the merged documents to a single new document, or **Mail Merge** to select a range of records to merge.

NOTES   If you have electronic mail or fax capabilities, you can merge a main document to an electronic mail address or a fax number in your data source file.

You can use databases created in other applications as the data source for a Mail Merge.

See Also   *Database; Mail; Open; Save/Save As*

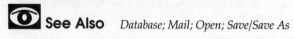

MARGINS

Margins define the distance from the edge of the paper to the beginning of document text. In Word, you can print between the left and right and top and bottom margins, or you can print some document items, such as headers or footers, in the margins. You can have more than one set of margins in a document that is divided into sections.

You can set document margins in Word by using the margin boundary markers on the Ruler or the Margins tab in the Page Setup dialog box.

To Set Precise Margins

By default, the margins in Word are set at 1 inch for the top and bottom, and 1.25 inches for the left and right. To set exact margin measurements, adjust the position of the header or footer, or create a binding offset, use the Margins tab of the Page Setup dialog box.

1.   Move the insertion point into the section of the document whose margins you want to change.

2.   Select File ➤ Page Setup, then choose the Margins tab in the Page Setup dialog box.

3.   Choose the margin options you want to reset. The options are described below.

4.   Select OK in the Page Setup dialog box.

OPTIONS

Top
Enter the distance from the top edge of the paper to the top of the first line of text.

Bottom
Enter the distance from the bottom edge of the paper to the bottom of the last line of text.

Left
Enter the distance from the left edge of the paper to the left edge of the line of text. If the Mirror Margins check box is selected, the text box is renamed "Inside."

Right
Enter the distance from the right edge of the paper to the right edge of the of text. If the Mirror Margins check box is selected, the text box is renamed "Outside."

Inside
Enter the distance from the left edge of the paper to the left edge of the text on the odd-numbered pages, and the distance between the right edge of the paper and the right edge of the text on the even-numbered pages in a document printed on both sides of the paper.

Outside
Enter the distance from the right edge of the paper to the right edge of the line of text on the odd-numbered pages, and the distance between the left edge of the paper and the left edge of the text on the even-numbered pages of a document that is printed on both sides of the paper.

Gutter
Enter the amount of additional space to allow for the binding margin of a document. If Mirror Margins is selected, the gutter is added to the Inside margin. If Mirror Margins is cleared, the gutter is added to the Left margin of the document.

From
Edge
Enter or adjust the distance for the position of the Header and the Footer in your document.

Apply To   Select the drop-down list, then choose the portion of the document whose margins you want to reset. You can choose Whole Document, Selected Text, This Point Forward, Selected Sections, or This Section.

Mirror   Changes the widths of the Inside and Outside
Margins   margins if you want to print on both sides of the paper.

Default   Changes Word's original default margins to the settings you usually use for documents.

To Set Margins with the Ruler

You can set the margins with the Ruler in either Page Layout view or Print Preview.

Move the mouse pointer to the margin boundary you want to change. The pointer appears as a two-headed arrow. Drag the margin boundary to a different measurement. If you hold down the **Alt** key while you drag the boundary, the margin's measurement appears in the margin area of the Ruler.

NOTES   The minimum margins you can set depend on the size of your paper and your printer.

If you have a large header or footer, the top and bottom margins settings will be automatically adjusted so the entire header or footer will be in the margin.

The indent is an additional distance between the left or right margin and the left or right edge of the text.

See Also   *Binding Offset; Headers and Footers; Indent; Page Setup; Ruler*

N E W

MASTER DOCUMENT

Use a master document to manage long documents. A master document is a file that contains subdocuments. You can open a subdocument and edit, rename the subdocument file, relocate the file, then save the changes to the subdocument, and the changes will also be updated in your master document.

Master documents can contain up to eighty subdocuments, and can be as large as 32 MB, not counting graphics. You must be in Master Document view to create a new master document or to turn an existing document file into a master document. The Outline toolbar and the Master Document toolbar appear when you are in Master Document view. You can switch to Normal view when you want to work with the whole master document.

If you create a template for your master document, it will override a different subdocument template except for special subdocument formatting such as columns, margin settings, and special page-number settings. You can apply styles or formatting to the master document or to any of its subdocuments.

Each subdocument is in a separate section of the master document. You can apply different headers and footers to each section of a master document.

To Convert a
Document into a Master Document

1. Open the document you want to change into a master document.

2. Select View ➤ Master Document to display the Outline and Master Document toolbars.

3. Use the Outline toolbar to arrange the headings in your document. By default, the built-in heading styles are applied to headings in your document.

4. Select the headings and text you want to include in subdocuments, then click on the **Create Subdocument** button on the Master Document toolbar. Each time Word finds the same heading level as the first heading level in the selection, a new subdocument will be created.

5. Save the master document. Each subdocument will also be saved as a file.

To convert a subdocument into master document text, select the subdocument, then click the **Remove Subdocument** button on the Master Document toolbar. The newly converted portion of the master document retains its section formatting.

To Create a New Master Document

1. Select File ➤ New and choose OK, press **Ctrl+N,** or click the **New** button on the Standard toolbar to create a new document.

2. Choose View ➤ Master Document to display the Outline and Master Document toolbars.

3. Type the master document's outline, and make sure the outline headings are in Word's built-in heading styles.

4. Select the headings and text you want to include in subdocuments, then click on the **Create Subdocument** button on the Master Document toolbar. Each time Word finds the same heading level as the first heading level in the selection, a new subdocument will be created.

5. Save the master document. Each subdocument will also be saved as a file.

To Delete a Subdocument

To remove a subdocument from the master document, select the subdocument icon and press the **Backspace** or **Del** key. You can then delete the file from your disk.

To Edit a Subdocument

Once you have created your master document, you can open any of the subdocuments and edit its contents. When you save the subdocument, the changes you made to it will be updated in the master document.

1. Double-click on the subdocument icon in the master document to open the subdocument file.

2. If necessary, close the master document to allow access to it by others.

3. Edit the subdocument as you would any other document.

4. Save the subdocument.

To Insert a
Subdocument into a Master Document

1. Select View ➤ Master Document to change to Master Document view.

2. Open the master document file.

3. Move the insertion point to the place in the master document where you want to insert a new subdocument.

4. Click the **Insert Subdocument** button on the Master Document toolbar. The Insert Subdocument dialog box appears.

5. Select the name of the file you want to insert in the master document in the File Name list box, then choose OK.

The document is inserted into the master document with its original file name. If the document is based on a different template or is formatted differently than the master document, the settings in the master document will be used in the subdocument when it is opened in the master document. The settings in the subdocument file will be used if you open the subdocument with File ➤ Open (**Ctrl+O**) or by clicking on the **Open** button on the Standard toolbar.

If you move the insertion point to the lower End of Section mark in a section, the new subdocument will be inserted in its own section as a separate subdocument. If you move the insertion point into an existing subdocument, the new subdocument will be a subdocument of the existing subdocument. Split the subdocument to place the new subdocument in the master document.

A master document can have up to eight layers of subdocuments.

To Lock a Subdocument

If you share the use of a master document with other people, you can lock subdocuments. A locked subdocument appears with a padlock icon on it, and can be opened only as a read-only file by anyone other than the author of the subdocument. The author's identity is taken from the Summary Info AUTHOR field code. However, anyone can unlock a locked subdocument.

1. With the master document open and in Master Document view mode, click on the icon of the subdocument you want to lock or unlock.

2. Click on the **Lock Document** button on the Master Document toolbar to lock or unlock a subdocument.

To Merge Subdocuments

1. If necessary, reposition the subdocuments to merge so that they are next to each other in the master document.

2. Click on the icon of the first subdocument.

3. Hold down the **Shift** key while you click on the icon of the next and any subsequent subdocuments.

4. Click on the **Merge Subdocument** button on the Master Document toolbar.

5. Save the master document.

The merged subdocuments are saved as a single subdocument of the master document. You can delete the individual versions of the subdocument files before they were merged.

To Move or Rename a Subdocument

You can save a subdocument to a different filename and location when you open the subdocument from within the master document. The link to the master document will be broken if you move or rename the subdocument without opening it from the master document. You can delete the earlier version of the subdocument if you no longer need it.

1. With the master document open and in Master Document view, double-click on the icon of the subdocument you want to move or rename.

2. Select File ➤ Save As. The Save As dialog box appears.

3. Type the new name for the subdocument in the File Name text box.

4. Choose OK in the Save As dialog box.

5. Select File ➤ Close to close the subdocument.

6. Save the master document.

To Relocate Subdocuments in the Master Document

You can rearrange subdocuments in the master document, or you can rearrange the headings in a subdocument. Begin with the master document open in Master Document view.

- Click on the subdocument icon to select the subdocument you want to reposition, then drag it to the new location in the master document.

- Select the heading you want to reposition in a subdocument and drag it to a new location in the subdocument or in another subdocument.

To Split a Subdocument

1. Select View ➤ Master Document, then open the master document that contains the subdocument to split.

2. Double-click on the subdocument's icon to open the subdocument.

3. Move the insertion point to the position where you want to split the subdocument.

4. Click the **Split Subdocument** button on the Master Document toolbar.

5. Save the master document.

NOTES Each subdocument you create is assigned its own file name based on the text of the first subdocument heading. However, if a file in the directory is already named what Word would normally choose, the subdocument is assigned a numbered file name based on the text.

See Also *Headers and Footers; Open; Outline; Page Numbering; Save/Save As; Section Layout; Styles; Summary Info; Template; View*

MENU

You can change the commands that appear on the drop-down menus to include the commands, macros, styles, fonts, and Auto-Text entries you use most often.

To Assign an Item to a Menu

1. Select Tools ➤ Customize, and choose the Menus tab.

2. In the Save Changes In drop-down list, highlight the name of the template where the menu changes will be stored.

3. Highlight the name of the menu bar command or other item in the Categories list box that contains the name you want to place on a menu.

4. Select the name of the item you want to place on a drop-down menu in the list box to the right of the Categories list box.

5. In the Change What Menu drop-down list, choose the name of the menu on which to place the selected name.

6. In the Position on Menu drop-down list, choose one of the options (described below) to position the new menu item.

7. If necessary, type a different name for the menu item in the Name on Menu text box. Type an ampersand (&) in front of the letter you want to use as a hotkey. Make sure there is not already an item on the same menu with the same underlined letter.

8. Select Add or Add Below.

9. Repeat steps 3–8 for each menu item you want to add to the selected template.

10. Choose Close in the Customize dialog box.

OPTIONS The options in the Position on Menu drop-down list are as follows:

(Auto)	Places the new menu item with related existing menu items.
(At Top)	Places the new menu item at the top of the menu commands.
(At Bottom)	Places the new item at the bottom of the menu commands.
Menu Items	Select the existing menu item below which you want to place the new item.

The other options on the Menus tab of the Customize dialog box are as follows:

Remove	Highlight a command in the list box beside the Categories list box, then select Remove to delete it from the list of menu items.
Reset All	Removes any changes and returns the menus to Word's defaults. Select Yes to confirm that you want to reset the menus.
Rename	Highlight a command or item in the list box, then type the name for the item in the Name on Menu text box. Select Rename to rename the menu item.

Menu Bar	Edits the items on the menu bar and displays the Menu Bar dialog box. Type the name of a menu you want to add, remove, or rename in the Name on Menu Bar text box. Type an ampersand (&) in front of the letter you want to underline in the name. Highlight the place on the menu bar where you want to insert the new menu name in the Position on Menu Bar list box. If you highlight an existing menu name, the new menu name will be positioned after the highlighted name. Select Add or Add After to add the name to the menu bar. Select Remove to remove the menu name highlighted in the Position on Menu Bar list box from the menu bar, then select Yes to confirm that you want to remove the item. Choose Rename to change the name of the menu highlighted in the Position on Menu Bar list box. Select Close in the Menu Bar dialog box, then choose Close again in the Customize dialog box. The changes you made will immediately appear on the menu bar.

To Use Shortcut Menus

If you have a mouse, you can use shortcut menus in Word for Windows to easily access commands that are associated with the task you are performing. For example, you can select from a variety of commands that are often used to edit text if you point to a paragraph and click the right mouse button. Shortcut menus are available for many different editing tasks including tables, paragraphs, embedded objects, and toolbars.

To use a shortcut menu, select or point to the item you want to edit on your screen, click the right mouse button, then highlight or click on the command in the shortcut menu you want to use.

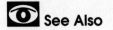 **See Also**   *AutoText; Font; Keyboard; Macros; Styles; Toolbars*

NEW

NUMBERING HEADINGS

To give a document structure, number the document headings to which you have applied one of Word's built-in heading styles. You can assign consecutive numbers throughout the document or assign new numbers to a document section.

To Assign or Customize Heading Numbers

1. Select Format ➤ Heading Numbering.

2. Choose the numbering format.

3. If necessary, select Modify to customize the format of the heading numbers. Choose any of the options (described below) in the Modify Heading Numbering dialog box, then select OK.

4. Select OK in the Heading Numbering dialog box.

After you have applied a numbering format to the headings in a document, you can remove the headings in the section that contains the insertion point by selecting Remove in the Heading Numbering dialog box.

 **OPTIONS**

Number Format	Change the Text Before and Text After of the bullet or number, and the Bullet or Number style. Choose Font to change the font and attributes of the text and bullet or number. Enter the starting number in the Start At text box. For each level after the first, choose the previous level formatting you want to apply in the Include from Previous Level drop-down list.

Number Position	Choose the Alignment of List Text in the drop-down list. Enter the distance between the left indent and the first-level text in the Distance from Indent to Text box, and the distance between the numbers and the text in the Distance from Number to Text box. Select the Hanging Indent check box to apply a hanging indent to each paragraph.
Restart Numbering at Each New Section	Starts each section with the number in the Start At text box.
Level *n*	Scroll to the level you want to customize, then use any of the options above to customize the format of the level. The changes appear as they are applied.

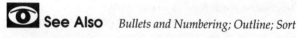 **See Also** *Bullets and Numbering; Outline; Sort*

OBJECT LINKING AND EMBEDDING

Many Windows applications, including Word, come with additional applications that use Object Linking and Embedding (OLE) to create and edit objects in your documents. Use OLE to embed graphics, equations, spreadsheets, and drawings in a document. You can edit an object you have embedded in the Word document.

To Create a New Object

1. Move the insertion point to where you want to embed the object.

2. Select Insert ➤ Object, then choose the Create New tab.

3. Select the kind of object to embed in the Object Type list box.

4. To display the object as an icon in your document, select the Display as Icon check box.

5. Choose OK in the Object dialog box. The application used to create the object opens on your screen.

6. Create the object.

7. To embed the object and return to your Word document, select the application's File ➤ Exit and Return to *Document* command, if it has one. Otherwise, click in the Word document outside the object.

To Edit an Object

1. Double-click on the object in your Word document; or select the object, choose Edit ➤ Object, then choose Edit.

2. Edit the object.

3. To update the object and return to your Word document, select the application's File ➤ Exit and Return to *Document* command, if it has one. Otherwise, click in the Word document outside the object.

To Embed a File

1. Move the insertion point to where you want to embed the object.

2. Choose Insert ➤ Object and select the Create from File tab.

3. In the File Name list box, select the file to embed.

4. To display the object as an icon in your document, select the Display as Icon check box.

5. Choose OK in the Object dialog box. The object is embedded in your document.

6. Save the document with the embedded object.

To Embed Part of a File

1. Move the insertion point to where you want to embed the object.

2. Open the source application and file, then select the data you want to embed.

3. In the source application, choose Edit ➤ Copy (Ctrl+C), then switch back to your Word document.

4. Select Word's Edit ➤ Paste Special command, and choose Paste.

5. Highlight the first item in the As list box that includes "Object" in its name.

6. To display the object as an icon in your document, select the Display as Icon check box.

7. Choose OK in the Paste Special dialog box.

To Modify the File Format of an Object

If an object is in a file format whose application you do not have, you can convert the file to the format of an application on your system.

1. Select the object whose file format you want to change.

2. Choose Edit ➤ Object, then choose Convert.

3. In the Object Type list box, select the file format you want for the object.

4. Choose Convert To to permanently convert the file format, or Activate As to temporarily convert the file format.

5. Choose OK in the Convert dialog box.

To Transform an Object into a Graphic

An embedded object appears as a picture of the data you have embedded. However, all the data is still in the object. To reduce the size of a file with an embedded object, you can convert the object into a graphic. The original data is no longer embedded in the object, and the object can be edited as a drawing.

1. Select the object you want to convert to a graphic.

2. Choose <u>E</u>dit ➤ <u>O</u>bject Con<u>v</u>ert.

3. Highlight Picture in the Object T<u>y</u>pe list box.

4. Choose OK in the Convert dialog box.

 NOTES   When you select the Displ<u>a</u>y as Icon check box, the Change <u>I</u>con button appears. You can select the icon that you want to display in your document in place of the object. Any changes you make in the Object dialog box appear in the Result area.

Embedded objects are the results of the {EMBED...} field code in your document.

👁 **See Also**   *Charts; Draw; Field Codes; Links*

OPEN

You can have as many open Word documents as you have system memory for.

To Open a Document On Disk

1. Select <u>F</u>ile ➤ <u>O</u>pen (**Ctrl+O**) or click the **Open** button on the Standard toolbar.

2. Type the path and name of the file you want to open in the File <u>N</u>ame text box, or select the name of the file in the File <u>N</u>ame list box.

3. Choose any of the options (described below) in the Open dialog box.

4. Choose OK.

OPTIONS

Dri**v**es	Select a different drive letter in the drop-down list.
Directories	Double-click on a different directory in the list box. The directory's files appear in the File **N**ame list box.
List Files of **T**ype	Choose a different file format in the drop-down list to change the display in the File **N**ame list box.
Find File	Displays the Find File dialog box.
N**e**twork	Displays the Connect Network Drive dialog box to connect to a network drive.
Confirm Conversions	Word asks for confirmation to use the suggested converter when opening a file created in a different format.
Read Only	Opens a file as read-only. Changes cannot be saved.

To Open a Recently Opened File

By default, the last four files you opened in Word are displayed near the bottom of the **F**ile menu. To open one of those files, select File ➤ **1**, **2**, **3**, or **4**.

To change the number of recently opened files that appear on the File menu:

1. Select **T**ools ➤ **O**ptions and choose the General tab.

2. Enter the number in the **E**ntries text box of the **R**ecently Used File List check box.

3. Select OK in the Options dialog box.

 **See Also** *File Management; Save/Save As; Windows*

OUTLINE

Switch to Outline view to display an existing document as an outline or to create a new outline. In Outline view, the Outline toolbar appears just above the document window, replacing the Ruler. Use the buttons on the toolbar to help create or edit an outline.

The headings in an outline are formatted with one of Word's nine built-in heading styles. You can change the style of a built-in heading with Format ➤ Style. Click on the **Show Formatting** button on the Outline toolbar to suppress the display of character formatting in your outline.

To switch to Outline view, select View ➤ Outline or click on the **Outline View** button on the horizontal scroll bar.

To Create an Outline

Apply one of Word's heading or paragraph styles to the text in an outline. Either select existing text and apply a style or select a style then type the text.

1. Switch to Outline view.

2. In an existing document, select the text to which to apply a heading or paragraph style. To create a new outline, type the text for the first heading and press ↵.

3. If necessary, choose one of the buttons on the Outline toolbar or use the shortcut keys in Table II.6 to change the heading level or paragraph style.

4. Repeat steps 2 and 3 for each heading and paragraph in your outline.

To Expand or Collapse an Outline

Use the Outline toolbar buttons to expand or collapse the text in an outline.

Table II.6: The Outline toolbar buttons and corresponding shortcut keys

Button	Key Sequence
Promote	Alt+Shift+← or Shift+Tab
Demote	Alt+Shift+→ or Tab
Demote to Body Text	Alt+Shift+5 (on numeric keypad)
Move Up	Alt+Shift+↑
Move Down	Alt+Shift+↓
Expand	Alt+Shift++ (plus sign on numeric keypad)
Collapse	Alt+Shift+− (minus sign on numeric keypad)
Show Heading N	Alt+Shift+n (1-8 on numeric keypad)
Show All	Alt+Shift+A or * (on numeric keypad)
Show First Line Only	Alt+Shift+L
Show Formatting	/ (slash key on numeric keypad)
Master Document View	—

- Move the insertion point into a heading and click the **Expand** button to expand one level of the heading's text or the **Collapse** button to collapse one level.

- Double-click the plus icon or the **Expand** button to expand all the text under a heading, or double-click the minus icon or the **Collapse** button to collapse all the heading text.

- Click the **All** button to expand all the outline's heading and paragraph text, then click the **All** button again to collapse the outline.

- Click on the **Show First Line Only** button to expand the first line of text into the whole paragraph, and click on it again to collapse the whole paragraph into the first line.

To Move, Promote, and Demote Headings

When you move, promote, or demote a collapsed heading, all the subtext is moved with the heading. In an expanded heading, select all the text you want to move, promote, or demote.

- Click the **Promote** button to move the heading or text to the left; click the **Demote** button to move it to the right.

- Click the **Demote to Text** button to change a heading into paragraph text.

- Drag the plus icon to the left to promote or to the right to demote the heading and its subtext.

- Drag the minus icon to the left to promote or to the right to demote the heading.

- Drag the paragraph icon to the left to promote or to the right to demote the subtext.

- Click the **Move Up** or **Move Down** buttons to move the heading or body text up or down.

- Drag the plus icon up or down to move the heading and body text up or down.

- Drag the minus icon or the paragraph icon up or down to move only the heading or the paragraph text up or down.

To Number Outline Headings

1. In Outline view, select Format ➤ Heading Numbering.

2. Select the numbering style to use in the outline. If necessary, select Modify to customize the heading numbers, then choose OK in the Modify Heading Numbering dialog box.

3. Choose OK in the Heading Numbering dialog box.

📝 **NOTES** The plus icon next to a heading indicates that the heading has subtext. The minus icon indicates that the head does not have subtext. A small square icon indicates text in a paragraph (subtext). Click on a heading's plus icon to select the heading and its subtext. Click on the small square icon to select only the subtext. Click between the icon and the heading to select only the heading.

Expand or collapse the headings and paragraphs in an outline so that the text you want to print is displayed on your screen, then print the document as usual. The plus, minus, and paragraph icons will not print.

You can quickly gather all the headings in an outline and insert a table of contents in your document with Insert ➤ Index and Tables.

👁 **See Also** *Numbering Headings; Outline; Print; Styles; Table of Contents; View*

PAGE BREAK

When a page is full, Word automatically inserts a soft page break and starts a new page in the document. If you edit the document, the soft page breaks are automatically adjusted.

To start a new page in your document, add a *manual* or *hard* page break. The hard page break will not be adjusted automatically when you edit the document, but you can delete it and insert another in a different location.

To Add a Hard Page Break

1. Move the insertion point to where you want to start a new page.

2. Press **Ctrl+↵**. Or select Insert ➤ Break, then choose OK in the Break dialog box.

To Delete a Hard Page Break

1. Click the **Normal View** button on the horizontal scroll bar, or select <u>V</u>iew ➤ <u>N</u>ormal. A hard page break appears as a horizontal line with *Page Break* on it.

2. Select the hard page break.

3. Press **Backspace** or **Del**.

NOTES You can use <u>E</u>dit ➤ <u>F</u>ind to find hard page breaks in your document, and <u>E</u>dit ➤ R<u>e</u>place to replace them with "nothing."

See Also *Keep Text Together; Page Setup; Repaginate; Section Layout*

PAGE NUMBERING

Page numbers you add to a document with <u>I</u>nsert ➤ Page N<u>u</u>mbers are placed in a frame in the header or footer. You can drag the page number to any position in the document, but it will expand the header or footer depending on the new location.

To Create Page Numbers

1. Place the insertion point in the section where you want to add page numbering.

2. Select <u>I</u>nsert ➤ Page N<u>u</u>mbers.

3. Choose any of the options (described below) to insert and format page numbers.

4. Select OK in the Page Numbers dialog box.

 **OPTIONS**

Position | Select Top of Page (Header) or Bottom of Page (Footer) in the drop-down list.

Alignment | Select where the page number will appear in the header or footer.

Show Number on First Page | Begins numbering on the first page of the document or section.

Format | Select the Number Format in the drop-down list. Select the Include Chapter Number check box to add the chapter number just before the page number. Highlight a style for the chapter number in the Chapters Starts with Style drop-down list, and choose the separator between the chapter and the page numbers in the Use Separator drop-down list. Select Continue From Previous Section to maintain consecutive numbers in adjacent document sections, or enter the number to begin the section's page numbering in the Start At text box. Choose OK in the Page Number Format dialog box.

To Delete Page Numbers

1. Move the insertion point into the section whose page numbers you want to remove.

2. Choose View ➤ Header and Footer.

3. If necessary, click on the **Switch Between Header and Footer** button, then select the page number.

4. Press **Backspace** or **Del**.

5. If necessary, click the **Show Previous** or **Show Next** button to select the page numbers in first page or even or odd headers and footers, and press **Backspace** or **Del**.

6.   Click **Close** on the Header and Footer toolbar.

 NOTES   Number the pages of a document before you divide it into sections. The headers and footers in each section are connected unless you break the connection with the Same As Previous button on the Header and Footer toolbar.

You can also apply character formatting to a selected page number in a header or footer. Apply a style to the page number if you want page numbers in all your documents based on the template to have the same format.

👁 **See Also**   *Headers and Footers*

PAGE SETUP

Use File ➤ Page Setup to change the margins, page layout, paper size, and the printer's paper source. The paper size and source options depend on the printer you have set up.

To Change the Paper Size or Source

1.   Select the text or move the insertion point to the section where you want to change the paper size.

2.   Select File ➤ Page Setup, then choose the Paper Size or Paper Source tab.

3.   Select the options (described below) to change the size or orientation of the paper and change options for printing the document.

4.   Choose OK in the Page Setup dialog box.

 **OPTIONS**

Pape_r_ Size   Select a predefined paper size, or select
                   Custom Size and define the height and
                   width of the paper.

_W_idth   Enter the width for a Custom Size paper.

H_ei_ght   Enter the height for a Custom Size paper.

Orientation   Change the orientation of the page to
                   Portra_i_t or Land_sc_ape.

_F_irst Page   Choose which printer tray or select Manual
                   Feed to define the paper source of the first
                   page of a section.

_O_ther Pages   Choose which printer tray or select Manual
                   Feed to define the paper source of the each
                   page of a section except the first.

_A_pply To   Select which portion of the document the
                   changes in the Page Setup dialog box will
                   apply to.

_D_efault   Changes Word's default Paper _S_ize or _P_aper
                   Source settings. Choose _Y_es to confirm the
                   change.

NOTES   When you change the page orientation, Word
automatically adjusts the Top, Bottom, Left, and Right margins.

See Also   *Alignment; Footnotes and Endnotes; Headers and
Footers; Indent; Line Numbering; Margins; Section Layout*

PARAGRAPHS

Each time you press ⏎ in a Word document, you insert a ¶ (paragraph mark) and start a new paragraph. To see paragraph marks on your screen, click the **Show/Hide ¶** button on the Standard toolbar. Formatting applied to the entire paragraph is stored in its paragraph mark. The formatting in one paragraph is automatically applied to the next paragraph.

To Create a Paragraph

Move the insertion point to where you want to end a paragraph, then press ⏎. The current paragraph ends, and the insertion point moves to the beginning of the next paragraph.

To Format a Paragraph

To apply a different format to an existing paragraph:

1. Move the insertion point into the paragraph or select the paragraph.

2. Use commands on the Format menu or buttons on the Formatting toolbar to change the paragraph's format.

To Set Paragraph Spacing

1. Move the insertion point into the paragraph or select the paragraph.

2. Select Format ➤ Paragraph, and choose the Indents and Spacing tab.

3. In the Spacing area, enter a measurement in the Before and After text boxes to indicate the amount of spacing you want before or after the selected paragraph.

4. Choose OK in the Paragraph dialog box.

NOTES To easily apply the same format to all paragraphs in a document, apply a paragraph style. By default, all paragraphs appear in Normal style in Word.

To start a new line without starting a new paragraph, press Shift+↵.

See Also *Alignment; Borders and Shading; Bullets and Numbering; Indent; Keep Text Together; Line; Line Spacing; Styles; Tabs*

PRINT

If you select and set up your printer in Word, your printer will print the document as it is displayed in Page Layout view or Print Preview.

To Print a Document

To print a document using Word's default options, click on the **Print** button on the Standard toolbar.

1. If necessary, select the portion of the document you want to print.

2. Select File ➤ Print (**Ctrl+P**) to display the Print dialog box.

3. Choose any of the options described below.

4. Select OK in the Print dialog box to print the document.

 **OPTIONS**

Print What	Choose Document to print the entire document; Summary Info to print the current file's summary information; Annotations to print only the current document's annotations; Styles to report on the styles in the current document; AutoText Entries to print the entries in the current and global templates; or Key Assignments to print the customized macro key assignments and descriptions for the current template.
Copies	Enter the number of copies to print.
Page Range	Indicate which pages to print. Select All to print the whole document; Current Page to print only the page the insertion point is on; Selection to print portions of the document you selected before you chose File ➤ Print; or Pages to print the pages you indicate. (Type 0 to print an envelope attached to the beginning of a document.)
Print	Select the order to print pages. Choose All Pages in Range to print the range of pages specified in the Pages text box. If you are printing on both sides of the paper, select Odd Pages or Even Pages.
Print to File	Select the check box then choose OK in the Print dialog box to print a document to a .PRN file so you can print the file on a different printer or a different system. Specify a name for the file in the Output File Name text box.
Collate Copies	If you have specified multiple copies, Word prints one entire copy of the document at a time.

To Set Default Print Options

1. Select File ➤ Print (**Ctrl+P**) and choose Options, or select Tools ➤ Options and choose the Print tab.

2. Select or clear any of the options (described below) in the Options dialog box.

3. Choose OK in the Options dialog box.

 **OPTIONS**

<u>D</u>raft Output	Prints a document with little or no formatting, depending on the selected printer.
<u>R</u>everse Print Order	Prints specified pages beginning with the last page. Clear the check box if you want to print an envelope.
<u>U</u>pdate Fields	Updates all fields before the document is printed.
Update <u>L</u>inks	Updates all links before the document is printed.
<u>B</u>ackground Printing	Lets you continue working in Word while your documents are being printed, but printing is slow.
<u>S</u>ummary Info	Prints the file's summary information on a page after the regular document text.
<u>F</u>ield Codes	Prints the field codes instead of their results.
<u>A</u>nnotations	Prints annotations on a page after the regular document text.
Hi<u>d</u>den Text	Prints the hidden text, whether or not it is displayed.
Drawing Objects	Prints objects created with Draw.
<u>P</u>rint Data Only for Forms	Prints only the form field results in a form.

Default <u>T</u>ray   Specifies the printer tray you want to use for all printing. (See *Page Setup* for information on how to change the tray for a single document section.)

 NOTES   Save a document before you print it in case of any kind of system error.

If you change printers, the same fonts may not be available on a different printer. Word automatically substitutes fonts in the document, but the spacing may be different. Check the appearance of your document before you print it.

👁 **See Also**   *Envelopes; File Management; Labels; Master Document; Page Setup; Print Preview; Print Setup; View*

PRINT PREVIEW

Use Print Preview to display a document exactly as it will be printed. You can edit and print the document in Print Preview.

To Display a Document

To switch to Print Preview, you can:

- Click on the **Print Preview** button on the Standard toolbar.
- Select <u>F</u>ile ➤ Print Pre<u>v</u>iew.

When you switch to Print Preview, the document is repaginated and its page numbers are updated, and the Print Preview toolbar appears.

To Edit and Print the Document

1. Switch to Print Preview and display the page you want to edit.
2. Click on the page to magnify it.

3. Click the **Magnifier** button on the Print Preview toolbar. The mouse pointer changes to an insertion point.

4. Click on the text you want to edit.

5. Edit the document, using regular editing techniques.

6. Click the **Magnifier** button, then click on the page again to return to the previous magnification.

7. Click the **Print** button to print the document.

8. Click **Close** on the Print Preview toolbar to return to the document window.

To Modify the Display

Use the buttons on the Print Preview toolbar, the vertical scroll bar, or the **Page Up** and **Page Down** keys to change the display.

• To magnify part of the document, click on the **Magnifier** button, then move the pointer to the location in the document and click.

• To display one page, click on the **One Page** button.

• To display up to six pages, click on the **Multiple Pages** button, then drag through the number and arrangement of the pages you want to display.

• To change the magnification of the pages displayed, select a magnification in the drop-down list or type a percentage in the **Zoom Control** text box.

• To display the Ruler, click on the **View Ruler** button. To hide the Ruler, click on the button again.

• To modify the font size so the document can be printed on fewer pages, click on the **Shrink to Fit** button.

• To hide everything on the screen except the document and the Print Preview toolbar, click on the **Full Screen** button. Click on the button again or press **Esc** to display all the screen elements.

• Click **Close** to return to the regular document window.

- Click on the next page or previous page buttons on the vertical scroll bar or drag the scroll box to scroll through the document. Or press **Page Up** or **Page Down** to scroll through the displayed document.

 **See Also**   *Margins; Print; Print Setup; Ruler; View*

PRINT SETUP

You must select and set up the printer you want to use before you print for the first time or if you change to a different printer. The capabilities of the printer you select affect how the document is displayed in Print Preview.

To Set Up the Printer

1. Select File ➤ Print (Ctrl+P), then choose Printer. The Print Setup dialog box appears.

2. Highlight the printer you want to use in the Printers list box, or choose Network to connect to a printer on the network.

3. If necessary, choose Options to select different settings for the printer. The available options depend on the printer you have selected.

4. Select Set as Default Printer.

5. Choose Close in the Print Setup dialog box.

6. If you want to print the document, choose OK. Otherwise, choose Close in the Print dialog box.

 **See Also**   *Print; Print Preview*

REPAGINATE

By default, Word adjusts soft pages breaks while you are editing your document. Background repagination is always on when you are in Print Preview or Page Layout view. You can speed up your editing in other views by turning off background repagination.

To Set Background Repagination

1. Click on the **Normal View** button on the horizontal scroll bar, or select View ➤ Normal.

2. Choose Tools ➤ Options, then choose the General tab.

3. Select Background Repagination to have Word adjust the pagination when you pause during editing a document.

4. Select OK in the Options dialog box.

NOTES Word always repaginates when you switch to Page Layout or Print Preview mode, and when you print the document.

See Also *Footnotes and Endnotes; Keep Text Together; Page Break; Page Numbering; Page Setup*

REPEAT

Characters you type and formatting changes you make to text are stored in Word until you perform any action other than moving the insertion point. For example, you can insert text you just typed anywhere in your document by selecting Edit ➤ Repeat Typing (**F4** or **Ctrl+Y**).

To Repeat the Last Edit

1. Move the insertion point to where you want to repeat the last edit.

2. Select Edit ➤ Repeat *Edit* (**F4** or **Ctrl+Y**).

 **See Also**   *Undo/Redo*

REVISIONS

You can mark revisions in a document to trace changes made to it by others. The changes made appear both on screen and in the printed document by default as underline and strikethrough characters. If more than one person revises a document for which you are marking revisions, their revision marks appear in different colors, with their initials and the date and time of the revision.

To Compare Versions

If you have two documents with different file names or in different directories, you can compare the documents and add revision marks.

1. With the edited document active, choose Tools ➤ Revisions or double-click on **MRK** on the Status bar.

2. Select Compare Versions. The Compare Versions dialog box appears.

3. Select the name of the original version of the document in the Original File Name list box, then choose OK. The changes made in the edited version appear as revision marks.

You can accept or reject revisions in compared documents as you do in a revised document.

To Mark Revisions

Once you turn on revision marking in a document, you can display or hide revision marks and change the format of the marks. Word keeps track of revisions even if they are not displayed in the document.

1. With the document whose revisions you want to track active, select Tools ➤ Revisions or double-click on **MRK** on the Status bar.

2. Select the Mark Revisions While Editing check box.

3. To suppress the display of revision marks on your screen, clear the Show Revisions on Screen check box.

4. To suppress the printing of the revision marks, clear the Show Revisions in Printed Document check box.

5. Choose Options to change the format of the revision marks, then select the options you want and choose OK in the Options dialog box. A description of the options appears below.

6. Choose OK in the Revisions dialog box.

 **OPTIONS**

Mark   Select the mark from the corresponding drop-down list for inserted and deleted text and for lines marking revised text.

Color   Select the color from the corresponding drop-down list for the inserted and deleted text and for revision lines.

To turn off revision marking in the document, clear Mark Revisions While Editing and choose OK in the Revisions dialog box.

To Merge Revisions

When others have added annotations or revisions to your document, you can insert their marked comments and revisions in the original document. The comments and revisions are assigned one of eight colors by Word. If you have more than eight reviewers, the same colors are used again.

1. Activate the revised document.

2. Select Tools ➤ Revisions, or double- click on **MRK** on the Status bar.

3. Select Merge Revisions. The Merge Revisions dialog box appears.

4. Select the name of the original document in the Original File Name list box, then choose OK. The revisions are merged into the original document.

If you sent a document by electronic mail and sent it to all reviewers simultaneously, double-click on the document's icon when the mail is returned. Select OK to confirm that you want to merge the revisions, then select OK again to merge the revisions into the original document. Repeat for each reviewer's document.

To Review Revision Marks

To see the proposed document revisions, you can review each revision and either accept or reject it.

1. With the revised document active on your screen, select Tools ➤ Revisions or double-click on **MRK** on the Status bar.

2. Select Review. The Review Revisions dialog box appears.

3. Choose Find → to move to the next revision, or ← Find to move to the previous revision.

4. To automatically move to the next revision, select the Find Next after Accept/Reject check box.

5. To include the proposed revision, select Accept. To remove the revision, choose Reject.

6. To change the acceptance or rejection of the last revision, choose Undo Last.

7. Select Hide Marks to suppress the revision marks in the document so you can see how it would appear if you accepted all the proposed revisions. Select Show Marks to redisplay the revision marks.

8. When you are finished reviewing the revisions, select Cancel or Close.

To accept or reject all the revisions without reviewing them first, select Tools ➤ Revisions or double-click on **MRK** on the Status bar, then select either Accept All or Reject All, and choose Yes to confirm the acceptance or rejection of the revisions.

NOTES You can also choose Tools ➤ Options, then select the Revisions tab to change the format of the revision marks.

See Also *Annotations; Document Protection; Mail; Print*

RULER

In Normal view, the horizontal Ruler is displayed by default under the toolbars. In Page Layout view and Print Preview, both the horizontal and vertical Rulers are displayed.

You can use the horizontal Ruler to set the first line indent of a paragraph, the left paragraph indent, and the right paragraph indent. You can also set the left and right document margins, add or remove tab stops in a paragraph, and adjust the widths of columns.

The vertical Ruler allows you to set top and bottom margins in your document.

To Display or Hide the Ruler

• Select View ➤ Ruler.

See Also *Columns; Indent; Margins; Paragraphs; Tabs; View*

SAVE/SAVE AS

Save your documents often as you are working. Use standard DOS filename conventions to name your Word files. Each file can have up to eight characters in its name, but cannot contain spaces or the * ?, .; [ ] + = \ /: | < > characters. Word documents are automatically assigned the .DOC extension unless you specify a different extension.

To Save All Open Files

Use File ➤ Save All to save all open documents and their templates, including the macros and AutoText entries attached to each template. If you haven't saved a document before, Word asks you to confirm that you want to save each before it is saved.

To Save a New File

The first time you save a file, the Save As dialog box appears.

1. With an unsaved document active on your screen, select File ➤ Save (**Ctrl+S**), File ➤ Save As, or click the **Save** button on the Standard toolbar. The Save As dialog box appears.

2. Type a name for the file in the File Name text box.

3. If necessary, select a different file format in the Save File as Type drop-down list.

4. To save the file to a different path, select a drive letter from the Drives drop-down list, then choose a directory in the Directories list box.

5. Select OK in the Save As dialog box.

To Save a Previously Saved File

Once you've saved a file, the Save As dialog box reappears when you select File ➤ Save As.

To save a previously saved document:

- Choose File ➤ Save.

- Press **Ctrl+S**.

- Click the **Save** button on the Standard toolbar.

To Set Save Options

You can customize the way Word saves your files with options on the Save tab in the Options dialog box.

1. Choose File ➤ Save As and select Options. Alternatively, select Tools ➤ Options and select the Save tab.

2. Select options (described below) for saving documents in the Save Options area. Clear options you don't want.

3. Choose OK in the Options dialog box. If necessary, select OK in the Save As dialog box to return to your document.

 **OPTIONS**

Always Create Backup Copy	Saves the current file on disk as the backup copy each time you save a file normally. Allow Fast Saves cannot be selected.
Allow Fast Saves	Saves only changes made to a document you are editing. Fast saves are not allowed over a network.
Prompt for Summary Info	Displays the Summary Info dialog box each time you save a new file.
Prompt to Save Nor-mal.dot	Displays the prompt asking if you want to save any formatting changes to the NORMAL.DOT template when you exit Word for Windows.
Save Native Picture For-mats Only	Reduces the size of a document file that contains a graphic imported from another platform, such as Macintosh.

Embed True-Type Fonts	Embeds TrueType fonts as pictures in your document. Others who open the document can view it with the fonts used to create the document even if they do not have the fonts.
Save Data Only for Forms	Saves data entered into a form's fields as a database record.
Automatic Save Every *n* Minutes	Saves all open documents automatically at the interval specified in the Minutes text box.

See Also *Annotations; Document Protection; File Management; Forms; Graphics; Revisions; Summary Info; Template*

SECTION LAYOUT

You can divide a document into sections. For example, if you have a document that consists of several chapters, each chapter could be in its own section. Each section in a document can contain its own formatting, which is saved in the section mark.

To Add a Section Break

When you add a section break, a section mark is inserted in your document. The section mark appears in either Page Layout or Normal view as a double-dotted line with *End of Section* on it. Neither the line nor the text will print.

1. Move the insertion point to where you want to insert a section break, then choose Insert ➤ Break.

2. Select one of the options (described below) in the Section Breaks area.

3.   Choose OK in the Break dialog box.

 OPTIONS

Next Page	Inserts a section break and begins a new section on the next page.
Continuous	Inserts a section break, but continues on the same page. This can be used to insert columnar text on a page with regular text.
Even Page	Inserts a section break and begins the next section on an even-numbered page.
Odd Page	Inserts a section break and begins the next section on an odd-numbered page.

To delete a section break, select the section mark and press **Backspace** or **Del**. Both the section break and formatting for the text above the section break are deleted, and the text takes on the formatting of the following section.

NOTES   You can use Word's Replace feature to find a section break and replace it with something else. Click the **Show/Hide ¶** button on the Standard toolbar to display nonprinting characters.

A section break is inserted automatically when you create columns, tables of contents, figures, and authorities, or an index in your document.

Apply formatting you want to use in all document sections before you divide the document into sections. Each section will contain the formatting applied to the entire document.

See Also   *Columns; Find and Replace; Headers and Footers; Margins; Page Setup; Page Numbers*

SELECT

Select text or another document item before you apply formatting, move, delete, copy, or change it in any way. Text you select is highlighted—the characters appear in reverse video. If you select a graphic or frame, eight handles appear around it.

To Select Document Items

Use the mouse or the keyboard to make a selection. Table II.7 shows how you can select document items.

Table II.7: Word for Windows selection methods

To select	With the mouse	With the keyboard
Any amount of text	Drag	Shift +← or →
One word	Double-click	Ctrl+Shift+→
A graphic	Click	↑ or ↓
One line	Click in left selection bar	Shift+End; Shift+Home
Multiple lines	Drag	Shift+↑; Shift+↓
One sentence	Ctrl+click	Shift+→; Shift+←
One paragraph	Double-click in left selection bar; triple click	Ctrl+Shift+↓; Ctrl+Shift+↑
Multiple paragraphs	Drag in left selection bar	Ctrl+Shift+↓; Ctrl+Shift+↑
Document	Triple-click in left selection bar	Ctrl+A
Vertical block of text except in a table cell	Alt+Drag	—
Screen down	Drag	Shift+Page Down

Table II.7: Word for Windows selection methods (continued)

To select	With the mouse	With the keyboard
Screen up	Drag	Shift+Page Up
End of document	Drag	Ctrl+Shift+End
Beginning of document	Drag	Ctrl+Shift+Home
Specific location	Drag	F8+↑, ↓, ←, or →

To cancel a selection, either press one of the arrow keys or click in the document window outside the selection.

To Set the Selection Option

You can drag to select part of a word. If you continue dragging into the next word, both words are automatically selected. You can turn off automatic word selection.

1. Select <u>T</u>ools ➤ <u>O</u>ptions and choose the Edit tab.

2. Clear Automatic <u>W</u>ord Selection.

3. Choose OK in the Options dialog box.

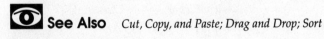 **NOTES** To select both text and graphics, move the insertion point to the beginning of the block you want to select. Then hold down **Shift** and click at the end of the block.

Double-click **EXT** on the Status bar to activate the **F8** (extend selection) key.

See Also *Cut, Copy, and Paste; Drag and Drop; Sort*

SORT

Rearrange text in a document by sorting it numerically, alphabetically, or by date. You can sort up to three types of information and perform a sort on paragraphs, lists separated by commas or spaces, and table rows.

Items that start with punctuation marks or other symbols (such as !, %, <<, or $) are sorted first, followed by items that start with numbers, then items that start with letters. Uppercase letters precede lowercase letters in the list. Subsequent characters decide the sort order if items begin with the same character, and subsequent fields decide the order if list items contain the same data in a field.

To Perform a Sort

1. Select the items to sort. If you are sorting a list, hold down **Alt** and drag to select the first character in each list item.

2. Select T**a**ble ➤ Sor**t** Text.

3. Select the options (described below) for your sort.

4. Choose OK in the Sort Text dialog box.

 OPTIONS

Sort By   Select the first type of data on which to sort text in the drop-down list. You can choose fields, columns, and paragraphs, depending on the selection in your document. In the T**y**pe drop-down list, choose Text, Number, or Date as the kind of data you are sorting. Select **A**scending (smallest to largest) or **D**escending (largest to smallest) as the sort order.

Then By	Select the second, and if necessary, third type of data on which to sort text in the drop-down list. Choose fields, columns, and paragraphs, depending on the selection in your document. In the Type drop-down list, choose Text, Number, or Date. Select Ascending (smallest to largest) or Descending (largest to smallest).
My List Has	Select Header <u>R</u>ow to disregard the first row of data while sorting a table. All heading rows are ignored in the sort. Or select No Header Ro<u>w</u> to sort all rows.
<u>O</u>ptions	Displays the Sort Options dialog box. To sort text outside a table, choose <u>T</u>abs or Co<u>m</u>mas as the separator character, or choose <u>O</u>ther and type the separator character in the text box. In the Sort Options area, choose So<u>r</u>t Column Only to sort a column of table data or text in a column, or <u>C</u>ase Sensitive to sort uppercase text before lowercase text. Choose OK in the Sort Options dialog box.

NOTES Tables are sorted by the characters in the first table cell. Numbered lists are automatically renumbered after a sort.

Sort the data in a data source before you perform the merge.

See Also *Mail Merge; Select; Tables; Undo/Redo*

SPELLING

Use the Spelling tool to catch typographical errors or misspelled words in your documents. You can create custom dictionaries to prevent special words not in the main dictionary from being questioned, and exclude dictionaries to question the spelling of words in the main dictionary.

To Check Document Spelling

1. Select <u>T</u>ools ➤ <u>S</u>pelling (**F7**) or click the **Spelling** button on the Standard toolbar. Each word that is not in the main or custom dictionaries, or is in the exclude dictionary, is highlighted in your document.

2. Choose any of the Spelling options (described below) for each highlighted word.

3. Choose OK to return to the document.

 OPTIONS

Not in Dictionar<u>y</u>	Displays the word highlighted in the document.
Change <u>T</u>o	Displays the spelling you highlight in the Suggestio<u>n</u>s list box. Or you can directly edit the spelling in the text box.
Suggestio<u>n</u>s	Displays a list of suggested words for the word in the Not in Dictionar<u>y</u> text box.
Add <u>W</u>ords To	In the list box, select a custom dictionary to which you want to add words highlighted by Spelling.
<u>I</u>gnore	Disregards the spelling of the word in the Not in Dictionar<u>y</u> text box.
I<u>g</u>nore All	Disregards the spelling of each occurrence in your document of the word in the Not in Dictionar<u>y</u> text box.
<u>C</u>hange	Changes the spelling of the highlighted word to the spelling in the Change <u>T</u>o text box.
Change A<u>l</u>l	Changes the spelling of each occurrence of the highlighted word in your document to the spelling in the Change <u>T</u>o text box.

<u>A</u>dd	Adds the word in the Not in Dictionary text box to the custom dictionary highlighted in the Add <u>W</u>ords To drop-down list.
<u>S</u>uggest	Displays a list of suggested words for the misspelled word in your document if you have cleared the A<u>l</u>ways Suggest check box on the Spelling tab of the Options dialog box.
AutoCo<u>r</u>rect	Adds the highlighted word to the list of AutoCorrect entries.
<u>O</u>ptions	Displays the Spelling tab in the Options dialog box.
<u>U</u>ndo Last	Restores the last change you made to the word highlighted in your document.
Cancel/Close	Closes the Spelling dialog box and returns to your document.

To Create a Dictionary of Excluded Words

Any words in the main dictionary are not questioned during a spelling check. If you want correctly spelled words to be questioned because you prefer a different spelling, create an exclude dictionary to be used with the main dictionary.

The exclude dictionary has the same file name as the main dictionary, but it has the .EXC extension. For example, if you are using the US English dictionary, the main dictionary file name is MSSP2_EN.LEX. The exclude dictionary associated with it will be named MSSP2_EN.EXC.

1. Click the **New** button on the Standard toolbar or press **Ctrl+N** to open a new document.

2. Type a word you want to exclude and press ↵ to start a new paragraph. Repeat for each word in the exclude dictionary.

3. Choose File ➤ Save (**Ctrl+S**) or click **Save** on the Standard toolbar.

4. Choose C:\WINDOWS\MSAPPS\PROOF as the location in which to store the exclude dictionary file.

5. Choose Text Only in the Save File as Type drop-down list.

6. Type a name for the exclude dictionary in the File Name text box.

7. Choose OK in the Save As dialog box.

To Create and Use a Custom Dictionary

If you often use technical terms or terminology that is questioned during a spelling check, create a custom dictionary that contains words that are not in the main dictionary. Words in a custom dictionary will be questioned only when they are misspelled.

1. Select Tools ➤ Spelling (**F7**) or click **Spelling** on the Standard toolbar, then choose Options. Or choose Tools ➤ Options and select the Spelling tab.

2. Use the options (described below) in the Custom Dictionaries area of the Spelling tab to create, edit, or remove a custom dictionary.

3. In the Custom Dictionaries list box, select the check box of any custom dictionary you want Word to use during a Spelling check.

4. Choose OK in the Options dialog box.

 **OPTIONS**

New   Create a new custom dictionary. Type a name
               for the custom dictionary in the File Name text
               box, then select OK in the Create Custom
               Dictionary dialog box.

Edit	Highlight a dictionary in the Custom **D**ictionaries list box, then select the button and choose **Y**es to open the custom dictionary as a document. Edit the dictionary, then save the document as a text-file and close the custom dictionary file.
Add	Add a custom dictionary file stored in a different path to the list box.
Remove	Removes the name of a custom dictionary from the list box.
Language	If you have created a custom dictionary to check the spellings of words in another language, select the language in the drop-down list.

To Set Spell Check Options

Customize Word's default Spelling options.

1. Select **T**ools ➤ **S**pelling (**F7**) or click **Spelling** on the Standard toolbar, then choose **O**ptions. Or choose **T**ools ➤ Options and select the Spelling tab.

2. Select or clear any of the options below.

3. Choose OK in the Options dialog box.

 OPTIONS

Suggest	Select the A**l**ways Suggest check box to have Word display suggestions for the spelling of misspelled words. Select From **M**ain Dictionary Only to display suggestions from the main dictionary.
Ignore	Select Reset **I**gnore All to remove all the words from the current session list for which you chose Ignore All. Select Words in **U**PPERCASE to have Word disregard words typed in uppercase letters. Select Words with Num**b**ers to have Word omit words that have numbers.

NOTES Use wildcards to check for the correct spelling of a word. The asterisk (*) represents any number of characters, and the question mark (?) represents one character.

Highlight a single word you want to check for spelling, then select Tools ➤ Spelling (**F7**) or click **Spelling** on the Standard toolbar. Then select No to return to your document.

See Also *AutoCorrect; Grammar; Language; Thesaurus*

SPIKE

To cut individual document items and paste them as a group, use Spike. You can cut multiple selections from your document and place them in Spike. Spike collects each item in sequence, separated from the next item with a paragraph mark. You cannot copy selections to Spike.

To see what Spike contains, choose Edit ➤ AutoText. Select Spike in the Name list box. Spike's contents appear in the Preview area.

To Add Data to Spike

1. Select the text or graphic you want to place in Spike.

2. Press **Ctrl+F3**.

3. Repeat steps 1 and 2 for each item you want to collect in the group.

To Paste Spike's Contents to a Document

- To use the contents of Spike more than once, place the insertion point at the beginning of the line or within spaces, and press **F3** or **Alt+Ctrl+V** to paste the contents of Spike into your document. Alternatively, type **spike** and click **AutoText** on the Standard toolbar.

- To paste the contents of Spike in your document and empty Spike, press **Ctrl+Shift+F3**.

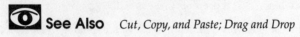 **See Also** *Cut, Copy, and Paste; Drag and Drop*

STARTUP PREFERENCES

Word's default settings for display, printing, editing, proofing, and other options are displayed on the tabs in the Options dialog box. These settings determine how Word appears and functions each time it starts. You can change the default settings for any of the functions in the Options dialog box at any time.

To Set File Storage Preferences

To change the default storage location of your Word documents, templates, and other items:

1. Select Tools ➤ Options and choose the File Locations tab.

2. Highlight the kind of file whose location you want to change in the File Types list box. The current location of each file type also appears in the list box.

3. Choose Modify.

4. If necessary, choose a drive letter in the Drives drop-down list and a directory in the Directories list box. Alternatively, select Network to connect to a network drive.

5. If necessary, choose New to create a new directory in which to store the items. Type a name for the directory in the Name text box and choose OK in the Create Directory dialog box.

6. Type the new location for the highlighted item in the Location of *Documents* text box. Choose OK in the Modify Location dialog box.

7. Select Close in the Options dialog box.

 **See Also** *AutoFormat; Cut, Copy, and Paste; Display; File Management; Grammar; Print; Revisions; Save/Save As; Spelling; Unit of Measurement; User Info*

N E W

STATUS BAR

The Status bar displays information about the current document or command, depending on the action you are performing.

To Display or Hide the Status Bar

Remove the status bar to display more of your document.

1. Select <u>T</u>ools ➤ <u>O</u>ptions and choose the View tab.

2. Select Status <u>B</u>ar to display the Status bar, or clear the check box to hide it.

3. Choose OK.

To Read the Status Bar

The following information can be found in separate areas on the Status bar:

Visible docu-
ment text

The page number based on the number that would be printed on the page, the section number, and the actual page number with the total number of pages in the current document appear in the first area at the left of the Status bar.

Position of the insertion point	The second area of the Status bar displays the exact location of the insertion point. The At measurement describes the position from the top of the page, Ln tells you the line of text, and Col tells you the character position within the line.
Time	Displays your system's current time.
Modes	The right side of the Status bar contains mode options. Double-click to toggle a mode on or off. An active mode appears in black letters, an inactive mode in gray. Choose **REC** to record a macro, **MRK** to mark revisions; **EXT** to extend a selection, **OVR** to type over text rather than insert it, or **WPH** to get WordPerfect help.

 NOTES When you select a command or a toolbar button, a short description of its function appears in the Status bar. If the command takes a while to complete, that information appears in the Status bar along with a graphic representation of how much of the action is finished.

See Also *Display; Insert/Overtype; Macros; Select; View*

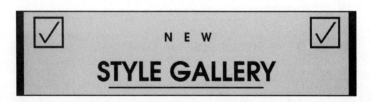

To add styles from a different template to an existing document, use the Style Gallery. You can see a preview of the way the document will appear when the styles in the new template are applied.

To Change the Document Template

When you use the Style Gallery, the styles in the selected template are copied to the document. The template's style takes precedence over the same style in the document. Any style in the template that is not already in the document is added to the document. Styles not in the template stay the same in the document.

1. With the document whose template you want to change active, select Format ➤ Style Gallery.

2. Highlight the template in the Template list box.

3. If necessary, select any of the options described below.

4. Choose OK in the Style Gallery dialog box.

 OPTIONS

Preview   Document displays the appearance of the active document when styles in the highlighted template are applied. To preview an sample document based on the highlighted template, choose Example. Or select Style Samples to preview a list of the styles in the highlighted template and samples of text formatted with the styles.

Browse   Change the directory.

You can also double-click on the name of the template in the Template list box to apply the styles to the active document.

To return to the document's original template, select Edit ➤ Undo or click **Undo** on the Standard toolbar.

 **NOTES**   Use File ➤ Templates to attach a new template to an existing document.

See Also   *AutoFormat; Styles; Template*

STYLES

Styles are named groups of formatting commands used to present your documents with consistent formatting. When you apply a style, each format in the style is applied simultaneously to selected text. Word comes with many built-in styles.

Word uses two types of styles—*paragraph styles* and *character styles.* Paragraph styles manage all formatting in a paragraph, including the font and size, line spacing, alignment, tab stops, and the borders and shading. Character styles are created using the options in the Font dialog box.

To Apply a Style

Use the Style drop-down list on the Formatting toolbar to easily apply styles in a document.

1. Place the insertion point in the paragraph or select the text to which you want to apply a style.

2. Select a style from the drop-down Style list.

You can also use options in the Style dialog box to apply a style.

1. Place the insertion point in the paragraph or select the text to which you want to apply a style.

2. Choose Format ➤ Style.

3. In the Styles list box, highlight the style to apply.

4. Choose Apply in the Style dialog box.

Paragraph styles appear in bold letters (character styles do not) in the Style drop-down list and the Styles list box.

Some of Word's built-in styles have assigned shortcut keys. They are listed in Table II.8.

Table II.8: Shortcut keys assigned to Word's built-in styles

Style	Key Sequence
Normal	Ctrl+Shift+N
Heading 1	Alt+Ctrl+1
Heading 2	Alt+Ctrl+2
Heading 3	Alt+Ctrl+3
List Bullet	Ctrl+Shift+L
Select a style	Ctrl+Shift+S
Apply the same style	Ctrl+Y
Remove a character style	Ctrl+spacebar

To Copy Styles

Copy styles from a document or template to a different document or template to save time and make sure the styles are exactly the same in both.

1. Choose Format ➤ Style, then select Organizer and choose the Styles tab.

2. Highlight the name of the style in the In *Document Name* list box. Press **Ctrl** as you select to highlight multiple names in the list box.

3. Select Copy to copy the selected style to the To *template* list box.

4. Choose any of the options described below to manage the styles.

5. Choose Close in the Organizer dialog box.

OPTIONS

Styles Available In/Styles Available In	Displays the name of the current document or its attached template.
Close File/ Close File	Closes the current file or template. The button changes to Open File.
Open File/ Open File	Displays the Open dialog box for opening a new document or template.
Delete	Deletes the selected styles from the document or template. Select Yes to confirm the deletion.
Rename	Highlight a style you want to rename or to which you want to add an alias, then select this button. Type a name in the New Name text box, or type a comma and an alias (for a built-in style), then choose OK in the Rename dialog box. Built-in styles cannot be renamed.

To Create or Modify a Style

To create or modify a style using formatting applied to existing text:

1. Move the insertion point into a paragraph, or select the text whose formatting you want to save as a style, then format the text as you want.

2. Click in the Style text box on the Formatting toolbar.

3. The name of the current style is highlighted. Press ↵ to modify the style, or type a name for a new style.

To create a new style or modify an existing style:

1. Choose Format ➤ Style, then select New or Modify in the Style dialog box.

2. Type a name for the style in the Name text box.

3. If you are creating a new style, select Paragraph or Character in the Style Type drop-down list.

4. In the Based On drop-down list, select a style similar to
the one you want to create.

5. In the Style for Following Paragraph drop-down list, highlight the style for a new paragraph typed after the style is
applied.

6. Optionally, select Shortcut Key and assign a key sequence
to the new style.

7. Choose Format, and then select the formatting for the style.

8. Select Add to Template to make the style available for any
document created with the same template.

9. Choose OK in the New Style or Modify Style dialog box,
then choose Apply in the Style dialog box.

You cannot have two styles in the same document with the same
name, but you can assign more than one name to the same style.
Style names are case sensitive, and can have up to 253 characters.
Do not place \ { } or ; in a style name.

A new style based on an existing style will also be updated when
you change the existing style.

To Delete a Style

When you remove a paragraph style from your document, any
paragraph with the style is formatted with Normal style. When
you remove a character style, the style is removed from any characters to which it was applied.

1. Select Format ➤ Style.

2. Highlight the name of the style in the Styles list box.

3. Select Delete, then choose Yes to confirm the deletion.

4. Choose Close in the Style dialog box.

To return a deleted style to your document, select All Styles in the List drop-down list in the Style dialog box. Or press **Shift** as you select the Style drop-down list on the Formatting toolbar.

To Display Style Names on Screen

In Normal or Outline view, you can display the names of paragraph styles on the left side of the window.

1. Select Tools ➤ Options and choose the View tab.

2. Enter a measurement greater than 0 in the Style Area Width text box to display style names. Type 0 in the text box to hide the style names.

3. Choose OK.

NOTES   You can redefine Word's Normal style. However, all new documents are based by default on the NORMAL.DOT template, and many existing styles in other templates are based on Normal style.

Assign shortcut keys to styles you use frequently. Click on the **Format Painter** button on the Standard toolbar to copy a style to selected text. Double-click on the **Format Painter** button to copy a style to multiple selections.

Select a template that contains the styles you want to use when you create a new document, then apply styles to all the document text. If a style is modified, all the text in the document to which the style is applied will also be changed.

To print a list of document styles and their descriptions, choose Styles in the Print What drop-down list in the Print dialog box.

Select only the text you want to copy to another document, not the paragraph mark. Otherwise, you will also copy the style applied to the paragraph to the other document.

Click the **Help** button on the Standard toolbar, then click on the text to display a message box with information about the formatting and styles applied to the text. Click the **Help** button again to remove the message.

 **See Also** *AutoFormat; Help; Print; Style Gallery; Template; View*

SUMMARY INFO

If you have added summary information to a file, you can use the information to search for the file or display the file's statistics.

To Add Summary Information

1. If necessary, select File ➤ Summary Info.

2. Type a title for the document in the Title text box.

3. Type the subject of the document in the Subject text box.

4. The name that appears in the Author text box is the name entered in the User Info dialog box. If necessary, edit it.

5. Type any words you may want to use when searching for the document in the Keywords text box. Separate keywords with spaces or commas.

6. Type document information in the Comments text box.

7. Choose OK in the Summary Info dialog box.

8. Save the file.

Each time you save a file with summary information, the statistics for the file are updated. You can display the file's statistics by choosing Statistics in the Summary Info dialog box.

To Set the Default Summary Info Option

To display the Summary Info dialog box each time you save a new file:

1. Select Tools ➤ Options, then choose the Save tab.

2. Select Prompt for Summary Info.

3. Choose OK in the Options dialog box.

 NOTES You can search for information entered in the Title, Subject, Author, and Keywords text boxes. The information in the Comments text box is for your use only.

Select Tools ➤ Word Count to display document statistics.

See Also   *File Management; Print; User Info*

SYMBOL

Use Insert ➤ Symbol to add a symbol or special character to a document. The symbols and special characters are not found on a standard keyboard, but can be printed.

You can also use Insert ➤ Symbol to insert a symbol or special character in the Find What or Replace With text boxes in the Find or Replace dialog boxes.

To Insert a Symbol or Special Character

1. Move the insertion point to where you want to insert a symbol or special character.

2. Select Insert ➤ Symbol to display the Symbol dialog box.

3. Choose either the Symbols or the Special Characters tab.

4. Select any of the options (described below) on the tab.

5. Choose Insert.

 **OPTIONS**

Font — Select the font you want to display in the Symbols Chart.

Symbols Chart — Select the symbol you want to insert. The shortcut key assigned to the symbol or the symbols ASCII key sequence is displayed in the Shortcut Key area.

Character — Highlight the special character to insert. The shortcut key combination assigned to the special character appears in the Shortcut Key area of the Character list box.

Shortcut Key — Display the Customize dialog box to assign a shortcut key to a symbol or special character.

 **See Also** *Find and Replace; Keyboard*

TABLE OF AUTHORITIES

Use a table of authorities to display a list of *citations*, or references to cases, rules, and statutes in a legal document. To create a table of authorities, mark the citation entries, then compile the table.

To Create Citation Entries

First, select the full text of a citation in your document. Subsequent entries of the citation will be a short version of the full citation. Citation entries are marked with a TA (table of authorities) field code in your document.

You can format the full text of the citation and the shortened text in the Mark Citation dialog box using formatting shortcut keys. The formatting you apply will only appear in the table of authorities. Formatting in the document text is not affected.

1. Select the entire text of the first citation in your document.

2. Press **Alt+Shift+I** to display the Mark Citation dialog box. The selected citation appears in the Selected Text and Short Citation text boxes.

3. Edit and format the text of the long citation in the Selected Text text box so that it appears the way you want in the table of authorities.

4. Choose a Category for the citation in the drop-down list.

5. If necessary, edit the text of the short citation in the Short Citation text box. It must match the text you want to mark in your document.

6. Choose Mark to mark a citation entry, or Mark All to mark all the citations in your document that match the long and short citations in the dialog box.

7. Select Next Citation to search for common text found in citations. Any text found is highlighted as the next citation in the document.

8. Select the text you want to mark as a citation entry.

9. Repeat steps 3–7 above to mark all the citation entries in your document.

10. Choose Close in the Mark Citation dialog box.

If you later edit your document and enter additional citations, select Mark All in the Mark Citation dialog box to update the citation entries.

To Create a Table of Authorities

After you have marked all the citation entries in your document, you can compile the table of authorities. The table is entered as a TOA field code in your document.

1. Move the insertion point to where you want to place the table of authorities.

2. Select <u>I</u>nsert ➤ Inde<u>x</u> and Tables, then choose the Table of <u>A</u>uthorities tab.

3. Select the category you want to compile in the Category drop-down list.

4. Choose any of the options described below.

5. Select OK in the Index and Tables dialog box.

 OPTIONS

Forma<u>t</u>s	Select one of the four built-in formats for the table of authorities, or select Custom Style, then choose <u>M</u>odify to create a custom format.
Use <u>P</u>assim	Substitutes *passim* in five or more page references to the same authority.
Keep Original Fo<u>r</u>matting	Uses the citation's document formatting in the table of authorities.
Ta<u>b</u> Leader	Highlight the character you want to use as the tab leader in the drop-down list.
Mar<u>k</u> Citation	Displays the Mark Citation dialog box.
<u>M</u>odify	Create a custom style for the table of authorities.

To Edit Citation Categories

You can replace the existing citation categories or create eight new categories to use when creating citation entries.

1. Press **Alt+Shift+I** to display the Mark Citation dialog box.

2. Select Category. The Edit Category dialog box appears.

3. In the Category list box, highlight the name of an existing category that you want to replace, or highlight a number from 8 to 16 to create a new category.

4. Type a name for the category in the Replace With text box.

5. Select Replace, then choose OK in the Edit Category dialog box.

6. Choose Close in the Mark Citation dialog box.

To Edit the Table of Authorities

The best way to edit the table is to change the citation entries in your document, then update the table of authorities. Move the insertion point into the field and press **F1** to display Help for the TA field code.

1. Move to the citation entry that you want to edit in the document.

2. To edit the text of the citation, change the characters within quotation marks (" ").

3. To delete a citation entry, select the field, including the field characters, and press **Backspace** or **Del**.

4. Add the necessary formatting switches to the field.

5. To update the table, move the insertion point into the table or field code and press **F9**. Alternately, select Insert ➤ Index and Tables and choose the Table of Authorities tab. Choose OK, then select Yes to confirm that you want to replace the existing table of authorities.

You can edit the text of the table of authorities. Press **Ctrl+Shift+F9** or **Ctrl+6** to change the TOA field to its results. However, if you later update the table, all your edits will be lost.

NOTES   If your document is extremely long, use a master document to work more efficiently.

See Also   *Field Codes; Font; Index; Master Document; Styles; Table of Contents; Table of Figures*

TABLE OF CONTENTS

A table of contents is a list of document headings and the pages on which they appear. You can have up to nine levels of table of contents headings in your document.

You can create table of contents entries in your document by applying styles to the headings or by inserting TC (table of contents) field codes. When you compile the table of contents, a TOC field is inserted in your document.

To Create a Table of Contents with Heading Styles

1. Apply one of Word's built-in heading styles to each heading to include in the table of contents.

2. Move the insertion point to where you want to place the table of contents.

3. Select Insert ➤ Index and Tables, and choose the Table of Contents tab.

4. Choose any of the options described below.

5. Select OK in the Index and Tables dialog box.

 OPTIONS

Formats	Select one of Word's six built-in table formats, or choose Custom Style to create your own style.
Show Page Numbers	Displays page numbers in the table of contents.
Right Align Page Numbers	Aligns page numbers along the right margin.

Show Levels   Enter the number of heading levels for the
                     table of contents.

Tab Leader   Highlight the character to use as the tab
                     leader in the drop-down list.

Modify   When Custom Style is the format, displays
                     the Style dialog box.

To Create a Table of Contents with Other Styles

1. Move the insertion point to where you want to place the table of contents.

2. Select Insert ➤ Index and Tables, and choose the Table of Contents tab.

3. Highlight the format for the table of contents in the Formats list box.

4. Select Options. The Table of Contents Options dialog box appears.

5. Make sure the Styles check box is selected.

6. Find the style in the Available Styles area you want to use for a table of contents level. Type the number of the level for that style in its TOC Level text box.

7. Repeat step 6 for each level in the table of contents. Highlight the level numbers for styles you do not want in the table of contents and press **Del** or **Backspace**.

8. Select OK in the Table of Contents Options dialog box, then choose OK in the Index and Tables dialog box to create the table of contents.

To return the table of contents heading styles to Word's defaults, choose Reset.

To Edit the Table of Contents

To edit the text in a table of contents, edit the text in the heading in your document. Then you can update the table of contents.

1.   Move the insertion point into the table of contents.

2.   Press **F9**. Or press **Shift+F10** or click the right mouse button and select Update Field. The Update Table of Contents dialog box appears.

3.   Choose Update <u>P</u>age Numbers Only, or Update <u>E</u>ntire Table.

4.   Select OK in the dialog box.

NOTES   You can also mark selected text in a document by inserting TC field codes along with any formatting switches. Then select the Table <u>E</u>ntry Fields check box in the Table of Contents Options dialog box and choose OK. Choose OK again in the Index and Tables dialog box.

See Also   *Field Codes; Index; Styles; Table of Authorities; Table of Figures*

N E W

TABLE OF FIGURES

Use a table of figures to list figures, illustrations, charts, slides, or photographs in the sequence they appear in your document. Generally, place the table of figures after the table of contents and before the document text. Create the entries for the table of figures with captions created using <u>I</u>nsert ➤ Cap<u>t</u>ion or by applying styles to the captions.

To Create a Table of Figures Using Captions

Use the following procedure to create a table of figures if you inserted captions with Insert ➤ Caption.

1. Move the insertion point to where you want to place the table of figures.

2. Select Insert ➤ Index and Tables, then choose the Table of Figures tab.

3. Highlight the type of label you want in the table of figures in the Caption Label list box.

4. Highlight the format for the table of figures in the Formats list box.

5. Choose any of the options described below.

6. Select OK in the Index and Tables dialog box.

 **OPTIONS**

Show Page Numbers	Displays page numbers in the table.
Right Align Page Numbers	Aligns page numbers along the right margin.
Include Label and Number	Includes the caption labels in the table.
Tab Leader	Highlight the character for the tab leader in the drop-down list.
Modify	If you chose Custom Style as the format for the table, select the button to customize the built-in styles.

To Create a Table of Figures Using Styles

1. Apply the same style to each caption.

2. Move the insertion point to where you want to place the table of figures.

3. Select Insert ➤ Index and Tables, then choose the Table of Figures tab.

4. Select Options.

5. Select Style, then highlight the style you applied to the captions.

6. Select OK in the Table of Figures Options dialog box, and again in the Index and Tables dialog box.

NOTES You can also mark entries with TC (table of contents) field codes. To compile the table of figures, select Options in the Index and Tables dialog box, then select the Table Entry Fields check box. Highlight a Table Identifier (the first letter of the caption labels) in the drop-down list, then choose OK in the Table of Figures Options dialog box and the Index and Tables dialog box.

See Also *Captions; Field Codes; Index; Styles; Table of Authorities; Table of Contents*

TABLES

Use tables instead of tabs in documents that contain columns of data, for text positioned in side-by-side paragraphs, or to present graphics beside text.

Tables are made up of rows and columns of data entered into cells. The cells' contents are individual paragraphs, and can be formatted with the same procedures.

To Automatically Format a Table

Use Table AutoFormat to apply predefined styles to a table, including borders and shading, and to automatically size the table.

1. Move the insertion point into the table or select the table.

2.   Choose Table ➤ Table AutoFormat.

3.   Highlight the predefined border and shading format for the table in the Formats list box.

4.   Choose any of the options described below in the Table AutoFormat dialog box.

5.   Choose OK.

 OPTIONS

Formats to Apply	Applies the Borders, Shading, Font, or Color specified in the predefined format. To make the table automatically adjust to fit its contents, select AutoFit.
Apply Special Formats To	Applies special formats to Heading Rows, First Column, Last Row, and Last Column, depending on the predefined format selected.

To Calculate Numerical Data in a Table

You can create simple spreadsheets in a Word table, and perform calculations on the table data.

1.   Move the insertion point into the cell where the calculation's results will appear.

2.   Select Table ➤ Formula.

3.   If necessary, type the formula in the Formula text box, preceded by an equal sign. To calculate the numbers using one of Word's built-in functions, select a function in the Paste Function drop-down list.

4.   Select a format for the calculation's result in the Number Format drop-down list.

5.   Choose OK in the Formula dialog box.

Cell references in a table are always absolute, and must be enclosed within parentheses in the formula.

To Change the Table Display

By default, table gridlines are displayed when you insert a table in your document. They are not printed unless you add borders to the table.

Select Table ➤ Gridlines to toggle the display of table gridlines.

You can display the end-of-cell marks, which indicate the end of each cell's contents, and the end-of-row marks, which indicate the end of each row by clicking the **Show/Hide ¶** button on the Standard toolbar.

To Convert a Table to Text

1. Select the table rows to change into paragraphs.

2. Choose Table ➤ Convert Table to Text.

3. Select Paragraph Marks, Tabs, Commas, or choose Other and type a character in the text box, to separate the text in each cell.

4. Choose OK in the Convert Table to Text dialog box.

To Convert Text into a Table

1. If necessary, add paragraph marks, tabs, or commas as separators.

2. Select the text you want to change into table text.

3. Click the **Insert Table** button on the Standard toolbar or choose Table ➤ Insert Table.

4. Alternatively, choose Table ➤ Convert Text to Table, choose any of the options below to change the selection, then choose OK in the Convert Text to Table dialog box.

OPTIONS

Number of <u>C</u>olumns	Enter the number of columns you want in the text box.
Number of <u>R</u>ows	Enter the number of rows you want in the text box.
Column <u>W</u>idth	Enter a measurement for the width of each column. If you select Auto, the columns are equal in width.
Separate Text At	Select <u>P</u>aragraphs, <u>T</u>abs, Co<u>m</u>mas, or choose <u>O</u>ther and type a separator character to define the columns in the table.

To Create a Table

1. Move the insertion point to where you want to place the table.

2. Click on the **Insert Table** button on the Standard toolbar, then drag to create a table with the corresponding number of rows and columns.

3. Alternately, choose Ta<u>b</u>le ➤ <u>I</u>nsert Table to create a table to your exact specifications. Choose any of the options described below, then select OK in the Insert Table dialog box.

 OPTIONS

Number of <u>C</u>olumns	Enter the number of columns you want in the table.
Number of <u>R</u>ows	Enter the number of rows you want in the table.
Column <u>W</u>idth	Enter the width of the columns. Select Auto to adjust the table columns evenly between the left and right margins.

Table Format	If you used AutoFormat to format the table, the name of the format appears in this area.
Wizard	Create tables in various formats.
AutoFormat	Automatically apply a predefined format to the table.

To Delete Cells, Rows, or Columns

To delete cells, rows, or columns, select the number you want to delete, then select Table ➤ Delete Cells, Rows, or Columns (depending on which you selected). If you selected cells, the Delete Cells dialog box appears. Select any of the options below, then choose OK.

 OPTIONS

Shift Cells Left	Moves the remaining cells to the left after the deletion.
Shift Cells Up	Moves the remaining cells up after the deletion.
Delete Entire Row	Deletes the row that contains the selected cell.
Delete Entire Column	Deletes the column that contains the selected cell.

To Insert Cells, Rows, and Columns

- To insert cells, rows, or columns in the table, select the number of cells, rows, or columns you want to insert, then click on the **Insert Cells** button, the **Insert Rows** button, or the **Insert Columns** button on the Standard toolbar, or choose Table ➤ Insert Cells, Rows, or Columns.

- With the insertion point in the last cell, press **Tab** to add another row at the end of a table.

- Select the end-of-row marks and click **Insert Column** on the Standard toolbar to add a column on the right edge of the table.

If you selected cells, the Insert Cells dialog box appears. Choose any of the options below, then select OK.

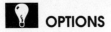 **OPTIONS**

Shift Cells Right	Inserts cells to the left of the selection.
Shift Cells Down	Inserts cells above the selection.
Insert Entire Row	Inserts rows and moves the selection down.
Insert Entire Column	Inserts columns and moves the selection to the right.

To Merge or Split Cells

You can merge two or more cells to place a heading in a table, or split a selected cell. When you merge cells, their contents are converted to paragraphs within the cell. Cells that you split are divided according to the number of paragraph marks. If there is only one paragraph mark, the text is placed in the left cell and empty cells are added to its right.

1. Select at least two cells to merge or one cell to split.

2. Choose Table ➤ Merge Cells or Table ➤ Split Cells.

To Modify the Column or Cell Width

To change the width of a column or cell, drag the column boundary to change the width of a column, or use Table ➤ Cell Height and Width:

1. Select the cells or columns whose widths you want to change.

2. Choose Table ➤ Cell Height and Width, and choose the Column tab.

3. Select any of the options below.

4. Choose OK in the Cell Height and Width dialog box.

 OPTIONS

Width of Column *Number*	Enter the width of the current selection.
Space Between Columns	Enter the measurement to specify the amount of blank space between the column boundaries and the cell contents.
Previous Column	Selects the previous column.
Next Column	Selects the next column.
AutoFit	Automatically adjusts the width of the column that contains the insertion point to its minimum width.

To change the column width with the mouse:

- Drag the column boundary. When you drag, the widths of columns to the right of the selection are changed in proportion.

- Hold down **Shift** while you drag to change the width of one column.

- Hold down **Ctrl** while you drag the column boundary to size all columns to the right proportionally.

- Drag the table column marker on the Ruler to size all columns to the right proportionally.

- Press **Ctrl+Shift** as you drag to change the width of the current column and the table.

To Modify the Row Height and Alignment

In Page Layout view, drag the row marker on the vertical ruler to change the height of a row. The size of the table changes proportionally.

You can specify the exact row height and set other row formatting options with Table ➤ Cell Height and Width:

1. Select the row you want to modify.

2. Choose Table ➤ Cell Height and Width, and choose the Row tab.

3. Change any of the options below.

4. Choose OK in the Cell Height and Width dialog box.

 OPTIONS

Height of Row *Number*	Enter the measurement for the height of selected rows. Select Auto to allow Word to adjust the height automatically. Choose At Least to specify a minimum row height, or Exactly to specify an exact row height.
At	If you choose At Least or Exactly as the Height of Row *Number*, enter the measurement in the text box.
Indent From Left	Enter the distance from the left margin to the left edge of the row.
Alignment	Choose Left to align the row along the left margin, Center to align the row between the left and right margins, or Right to align the row along the right margin.
Allow Row to Break Across Pages	Lets a table split across a page break at the selected row.

| Previous Row | Selects the previous row. |
| Next Row | Selects the next row. |

To Number Table Cells

1. Select the cells you want to number.

2. Click the **Numbering** button on the Standard toolbar. The Table Numbering dialog box appears.

3. Choose any of the options below to number the table.

4. Choose OK in the Table Numbering dialog box.

 **OPTIONS**

Number Across Rows	Numbers selected cells from left to right across the rows, row by row.
Number Down Columns	Numbers selected cells from top to bottom, column by column.
Number Each Cell Only Once	Numbers each cell rather than each paragraph within a cell.

To Repeat Table Headings

Table headings are not automatically repeated across page breaks. You can have Word repeat the headings in tables that span more than one page, and automatically update edited heading text.

1. Select the row or rows, starting with the first table row, that contain the text you want to use as headings.

2. Choose Table ➤ Headings.

Headings are not repeated or updated in tables that contain hard page breaks.

To Select Cells, Rows, Columns, or Data

To select items in a table:

- Drag over text in a cell to select the text.

- Click the cell selection bar on the left side of the cell to select the cell.

- Click the row selection bar on the left side of the row or choose Table ➤ Select Row to select the row.

- Click the top gridline or choose Table ➤ Select Column to select a column.

- Hold down **Shift** while you click another cell, row, or column to extend the selection.

- Choose Table ➤ Select Table (**Alt+Num 5**) to select the entire table.

- Press **Tab** to select the contents of the next cell, or **Shift+Tab** to select the contents of the previous cell.

- To extend a selection, hold down **Shift** while pressing ↑, ↓, ← or →.

To Split a Table

Split the table if you want to place text or a graphic between table rows. A paragraph mark is inserted where the table is split.

1. Move the insertion point into a cell in the row where you want the second table to begin.

2. Select Table ➤ Split Table. (Or press **Ctrl+Shift+Enter**.)

To reunite the table, delete the paragraph mark.

NOTES Add captions to tables with Insert ➤ Captions. Then the captions will automatically be updated if you change the tables.

Tab moves the insertion point to the next cell in the table or adds a row at the end of the table. Set tab stops with the Ruler or the Tabs command. The measurements you enter in the Tabs dialog box are relative to the margin of the cell, not the margin of the page. To insert a tab character in a cell, press **Ctrl+Tab**.

👁 **See Also**   *Borders and Shading; Bullets and Numbering; Captions; Columns; Cut, Copy, and Paste; Paragraphs; Ruler; Sort; Tabs; View*

TABS

By default, tab stops are set at each 0.5 inch between the left and right margins. To move to the next tab stop, press **Tab** to insert a tab character. Click the **Show/Hide ¶** button on the Standard toolbar to display tab characters on your screen.

To Set Tab Stops

Use **Tab Alignment** on the Ruler or F<u>o</u>rmat ➤ <u>T</u>abs to set tab stops.

To set tabs on the Ruler:

1. Select the paragraph whose tab stops you want to change.

2. Click **Tab Alignment** at the left end of the Ruler to select the type of tab stop you want to place on the Ruler. As you click, the button cycles through left-aligned, center aligned, right-aligned, and decimal tab stops.

3. Click on the Ruler where you want to place the tab stop.

To precisely define tab stops:

1. Select the paragraph whose tab stops you want to set.

2. Select F<u>o</u>rmat ➤ <u>T</u>abs. The Tabs dialog box appears.

3. Choose any of the options described below.

4. Choose OK in the Tabs dialog box.

 **OPTIONS**

Tab Stop Position	Type a new tab stop in the text box, or select an existing tab stop from the list box.
Default Tab Stops	Enter the measurement to reset the default tab stops for the entire document.
Alignment	Choose Left to align the text to the right at the tab stop, Center to align the text at the center, Right to align the text to the left, Decimal to align a decimal, or Bar to place a vertical bar at the tab stop.
Leader	Select the character to use as a tab leader.
Set	Set a selected tab stop.
Clear	Clear a selected tab stop.
Clear All	Clear all tab stops except the defaults.

See Also *Indent; Margins; Paragraphs; Ruler*

TEMPLATE

You can save in a template the styles, formatting, and text that you use in similar documents, and place AutoText entries and macros used for similar documents in the template. To create a document of that type, open a new document based on the template.

To Create a Document with a Template

By default, all new documents are created with the NORMAL.DOT template. You can choose a different template if you wish.

1. Select File ➤ New.

2. Highlight the template on which to base the new document in the Template list box.

3. Choose OK in the New dialog box.

To Create a New Template

1. Select File ➤ New.

2. Choose Template in the New area of the dialog box.

3. Select OK.

4. Type any text, create any macros or AutoText entries, define the page setup, customize the toolbars or menus, and
create any styles necessary for your document.

5. Choose File ➤ Save (**Ctrl+S**) or click the **Save** button on
the Standard toolbar.

6. Type a name for the template in the File Name text box.
The .DOT extension is added automatically.

7. Choose OK in the Save As dialog box.

To Edit a Template

1. Select File ➤ Open (**Ctrl+O**) or click the **Open** button on
the Standard toolbar.

2. Choose Document Templates (*.dot) in the List Files of
Type list box.

3. If necessary, change the directory to C:\WINWORD\
TEMPLATE.

4. Highlight the template to edit in the File Name list box.

5. Choose OK in the Open dialog box.

6. Edit the template as you would a regular document.

7. Save the template.

To Manage Templates

You can attach a different template to the active document, copy template items to other templates, or customize template items.

1. Choose File ➤ Templates.

2. Choose the appropriate options (described below), to manage your document template.

3. Select OK in the Templates dialog box.

 OPTIONS

Document Template	Type the name of the template you want to attach to the current document. Or select Attach, highlight the name of the template in the File Name list box, then choose OK. Select Automatically Update Document Styles to replace the styles in the current document with those of the same name in the attached template.
Global Templates and Add-ins	Select the check box of any template in the list box you want to be available whenever you start Word for Windows. Choose Add, then select the name of a template and choose OK to add it to the list box. Highlight the name of a template in the list box, then choose Remove to delete it from the global list.
Organizer	Display the Organizer dialog box. You can copy styles, macros, AutoText, and toolbars to other documents or templates. You can rename or delete styles, macros, AutoText, and toolbars within documents or templates.

 **NOTES**   Word's templates are stored by default in the C:\WINWORD\TEMPLATE directory.

Copy styles from another document with Style Gallery.

See Also   *AutoText; Macros; Style Gallery; Styles*

Each time you start Word for Windows, the Tip of the Day dialog box appears. The dialog box includes tips on using Word more efficiently and humorous tips on life in general.

To Control the Display of the Tip of the Day

- To display the Tip of the Day dialog box while you are working in Word, select Help ➤ Tip of the Day.

- To view the next tip, select Next Tip.

- To display a list of available tips by category, select More Tips.

- To suppress the display of the dialog box when you start Word, clear the Show Tips at Startup check box.

- Choose OK in the Tip of the Day dialog box to return to the document window.

See Also   *Help*

THESAURUS

Use Word's built-in Thesaurus to find synonyms or antonyms for a selected word or phrase.

To Use the Thesaurus

1. If necessary, select a word or phrase you want to look up.

2. Choose Tools ➤ Thesaurus (**Shift+F7**). The Thesaurus dialog box appears.

3. Perform any of the actions listed in *Options* below.

 OPTIONS

Looked Up	Displays the word you want to look up, whether it was typed in the text box, selected in your document, or selected in the Meanings or the Replace with Synonym list box. Choose a word in the drop-down list to review meanings and synonyms for each displayed word.
Meanings	Displays the meanings of the word in the Looked Up text box.
Replace with Synonym	Displays synonyms of the item highlighted in the Meanings list box. The word in the text box will replace a selected word in your document if you choose Replace.
Insert	Type the word you want to look up in the text box if you do not select a word when you activate Thesaurus.
Replace	Replaces the word in your document with the word in the Replace with Synonym text box.

Look Up	Looks up the highlighted word in the Looked Up, Insert, or Replace with Synonym text box.
Cancel	Closes the Thesaurus.
Previous	Displays the last word looked up and its meanings.

 **See Also** *Grammar; Spelling*

NEW

TOOLBAR

You can customize Word's built-in toolbars or create entirely new toolbars. Toolbar buttons can contain commands, macros, AutoText entries, fonts, and styles for easy access. If necessary, you can create buttons for the items you want to place on the toolbar.

To Create or Edit Toolbars

1. Select View ➤ Toolbars (or right-click on a displayed toolbar and select Toolbars).

2. Choose any of the options (described below) in the Toolbars dialog box.

3. Select OK to return to your document.

OPTIONS

Toolbars	Select the check box of any toolbar you want to display in the list box.

New | Type a name for the toolbar in the Toolbar Name text box. Select the template in which to store the toolbar in the Make Toolbar Available To list box, then choose OK.

Reset/Delete | Highlight a built-in toolbar then choose Reset and select OK to return it to its original defaults. If you highlight a custom toolbar, Reset becomes Delete. Select the button, then choose Yes to confirm the deletion of the toolbar.

Color Buttons | Colors the toolbar buttons.

Large Buttons | Displays larger toolbar buttons.

Show ToolTips | Displays the description of a button's function when the mouse pointer is on it.

To Customize a Toolbar

1. Display the toolbar which you want to customize.

2. Select Tools ➤ Customize and choose the Toolbars tab (or right-click on a displayed toolbar and select Customize).

3. Select the template where you want to save the changes in the Save Changes In drop-down list.

4. Perform any of the actions described in *Options* below.

5. Select Close to return to your document.

 **OPTIONS**

Add a Button | Select an item in the Categories list box. If the item has built-in buttons, they are displayed in the Buttons area. Click on a button to see a description of its function. Drag the button from the box to the right of the Categories list box to the location on the toolbar.

Delete a Button	Drag the button off the toolbar.
Move a Button	Drag the button to a different location or toolbar.
Copy a Button	Press **Ctrl** while dragging the button to a different location or toolbar.
Customize a Button	Select All Commands, Macros, Fonts, AutoText, or Styles in the Categories list box. Drag the item from the box next to the Categories list box to the toolbar—the Custom Button dialog box appears. Click on a button, or type text you want to appear on the button in the Text Button Name text box. Select Edit to customize the button, or Assign to place the text or graphic on the blank button on the toolbar.

 **NOTES** To display a list of available toolbars, move the mouse pointer to a toolbar and click the right button. Select the toolbar you want to display on screen.

Drag a toolbar anywhere on your screen. You can also place them vertically along the left or right edge of the window or resize a floating toolbar.

See Also *Menus; Template*

Word tracks your last few editing changes. Use Undo to reverse the last several actions you performed, and Redo to reverse an action you canceled.

- To reverse your last action, choose <u>E</u>dit ➤ <u>U</u>ndo (**Ctrl+Z**) or click the **Undo** button on the Standard toolbar.

- To reverse your last several actions, select the **Undo** drop-down list on the Standard toolbar, then select the action to undo.

- To reverse the last undo, select <u>E</u>dit ➤ <u>R</u>edo (**F4** or **Ctrl+Y**) or click the **Redo** button on the Standard toolbar.

- To reverse the last several cancellations, click on the **Redo** drop-down list on the Standard toolbar, then select the action you want to reverse.

 **See Also**   *Repeat*

UNIT OF MEASUREMENT

By default, Word uses inches as the unit of measurement. You can specify any of the units in Table II.9 as the unit of measurement when a measurement is entered in a dialog box. Or you can change the default unit of measurement.

To Set the Default Unit of Measurement

1. Select <u>T</u>ools ➤ <u>O</u>ptions and choose the General tab.

2. Highlight the unit in the <u>M</u>easurement Units drop-down list.

3. Choose OK in the Options dialog box.

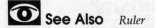 **See Also**   *Ruler*

Table II.9: Units of measurement

Unit	Abbreviation	Equal To
centimeter	cm	2.54 = 1 inch
inch	in or "	72 points or 6 picas
line	li	12 points
pica	pi	12 points
point	pt	1 line
Em	Em	Size of font

USER INFO

Information about the person who uses Word appears on the User Info tab of the Options dialog box. The items displayed are inserted as the return address for envelopes and labels, the author of a file, and the initials used when creating annotations.

To Edit the User Information

1. Choose Tools ➤ Options and select the User Info tab.

2. Type the name you want to appear in the AUTHOR field of a file's summary information in the Name text box.

3. Type the initials you want to use for your annotations in the Initials text box.

4. If necessary, type the information for the return address on envelopes or labels in the Mailing Address text box.

5. Choose OK in the Options dialog box.

 **NOTES** If you have already used <u>T</u>ools ➤ <u>E</u>nvelopes and Labels, the correct return address should be in the <u>M</u>ailing Address text box.

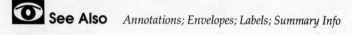 **See Also** *Annotations; Envelopes; Labels; Summary Info*

VIEW

Use any of Word's six views to work in your documents.

To Change the View

Each view is designed for a specific task, described in *Options* below.

- Click the **Normal View**, **Page Layout View**, or **Outline View** button on the horizontal scroll bar.

- Click the **Print Preview** button on the Standard toolbar.

- Choose <u>V</u>iew ➤ <u>N</u>ormal, <u>O</u>utline, <u>P</u>age Layout, <u>M</u>aster Document, or F<u>u</u>ll Screen.

- Select <u>F</u>ile ➤ Print Pre<u>v</u>iew.

 **OPTIONS**

Normal	For creating and editing documents. Allows you to work faster than other views.
Outline	For collapsing an existing document to display only headings, or creating a new outline and automatically applying heading styles.

Page Layout	For displaying a document just as it will appear when printed.
Master Document	For organizing subdocuments into a large document.
Full Screen	For removing all toolbars, menus, scroll bars, Rulers, and the Status bar from the screen so that you can see more of your document. Press **Esc** or click the **Full Screen** button to display the screen items.
Print Preview	For displaying the document page by page to see exactly how it will appear when printed.

 See Also   *Master Document; Outline; Print Preview*

To repeat text or a graphic on every page of a document, use a *watermark* in a header or footer. A watermark will be printed where you place it; it is not restricted to the header or footer.

To Create a Watermark

1. Click the **Drawing** button on the Standard toolbar.

2. Select View ➤ Header and Footer.

3. Click the **Show/Hide Document Text** button on the Header and Footer toolbar to hide the document text.

4. Draw the object or create a text box and type the text you want to appear as a watermark.

5. Select the object, then click the **Send Behind Text** button on the Drawing toolbar.

6. Choose the **Close** button on the Header and Footer toolbar to return to your document.

 NOTES To make a watermark from an imported graphic, create a text box, then use **Cut** and **Paste** to position the graphic in the text box.

See Also *Draw; Headers and Footers*

WINDOWS

You can have as many documents open in Word as your system's memory will allow. Use the commands on the Window menu to manage open documents in Word.

To Manage Document Windows

- To display a different part of the current document, choose Window ➤ New Window. Any changes you make to one window of a document will also appear in other open windows.

- To display all open windows on your screen, choose Window ➤ Arrange All.

- To divide the active window into two panes, choose Window ➤ Split. A horizontal gray line appears. Move the mouse to position the line where you want to split the screen, then click the mouse button.

- Alternatively, double-click the split box above the vertical scroll bar to split a window into panes.

- To move between panes, click in the pane where you want to edit, or press **F6** to move back and forth between the panes.

- Select <u>W</u>indow ➤ *n* to choose a different active window.

 **See Also** *Charts*

Use wizards to help you create and format documents, tables, letters, and memos. When you select a wizard and answer its questions, it sets up a basic document for you to use.

To Create a Document with a Wizard

1. Choose <u>F</u>ile ➤ <u>N</u>ew.

2. Highlight one of the Wizard templates in the <u>T</u>emplate list box.

3. Choose OK in the New dialog box. The wizard's dialog box appears.

4. Answer the questions and select the necessary options to set up your document layout. Select <u>N</u>ext to display the next set of options for the document, or <u>B</u>ack to return to the previous options.

5. Choose <u>F</u>inish to create the specified document.

 **See Also** *Table; Template*

ZOOM

Change the magnification of the display of a document on screen with the **Zoom Control** box on the Standard toolbar or View ➤ Zoom.

To Change the Magnification

- Click the **Zoom Control** drop-down list on the Standard toolbar, then select the magnification you want in the list.

- Select the percentage in the **Zoom Control** text box on the Standard toolbar, then type a different number.

- Choose View ➤ Zoom, then select a predefined option or enter the percentage in the Percent text box. Choose OK in the Zoom dialog box.

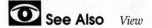 **See Also** *View*

Index

About This Index: Page numbers shown in **boldface** indicate principal discussions of topics and subtopics.

A

abbreviations, **14–16**
active modes, 204
adding. *See also* inserting
  annotations, **10–11**
  captions, **33–35**
  frames, **100**
  line numbers, **133–134**
  newspaper columns, **40**
  notes, **89–91**
  page breaks, **172**
  sections, **191–192**
  Spelling dictionaries, 200
  Spelling dictionary words, 198
  summary information, **211**
  toolbar buttons, 238
addresses
  on envelopes, **64–65**
  on labels, 130
  on mail, 145
aligning
  columns, 40
  drawing objects, 61
  indexes, 122
  lists, 32
  page numbers, 174
  rows, 228
  tab stops, 232
  tables of contents, 217
  tables of figures, 220
  text, **8–9**
All Caps fonts, 87

ampersands (&) in file searches, 77
AND operators
  in databases, 47
  in file searches, 77
annotations
  copying, **11**
  deleting, **11–12**
  editing, **11**
  for help text, 113
  hiding marks for, **12**
  merging, **146**
  new features in, 2
  playing back, **13**
  printing, **12**, 179–180
  in protected documents, 56–57
  text, **10**, **13**
  viewing, **13**
  voice, **10–11**, **13**
antonyms, **236–237**
appearance. *See* formatting; styles
applying
  borders and shading, **27–29**
  fonts, **85–88**
  styles, **206–207**
ascending sorts, 47, 195
assigning menu items, **160–162**
asterisks (*)
  in file searches, 73–74, 77–78
  in spell checking, 201
at signs (@) in file searches, 78
attaching templates, 234

authors
  entering, 211
  in file searches, 75
AutoCaption feature, **33–34**
AutoCorrect feature, **13**
  creating entries for, **14–15**
  deleting entries in, **15**
  editing entries in, **15–16**
  new features in, 2
  for spelling errors, **14**
AutoFormat feature, **16**
  for formatting text, **17**
  new features in, 2
  options for, **18–20**
  reviewing changes made by,
    17–18
automatic hyphenation,
    115–116
automatic operations. *See*
    macros
automatic saves, 191
AutoText feature
  creating entries for, **20**
  deleting entries for, **21**
  editing entries for, **21**
  inserting entries with, **22**
  names of entries for, **20–21**
  new features in, 2
  printing entries for, **22**

B

background color, 29
background printing, 180
background repagination, **184**
backslashes (\) in file searches,
    77–78
backups when saving, 190
balanced columns, 41
bar codes
  on envelopes, 65

  on labels, 130
binding offsets, **23–24**
.BMP files, 138
Bold font, 85
bookmarks
  calculations with, **26–27**
  creating, **24**
  for cross-references, 43
  deleting, **24–25**
  displaying, **25**
  editing, **25–26**
  for form fields, 97
  for help, 112
  for indexes, 123
  moving, **26**
borders
  applying, **27–29**
  for dropped capitals, 63
  for graphics, 106
  predefined, **29**
breaking links, 141
British spelling, checking, 132
browse buttons, xx
bullets
  with AutoFormat, 19
  on lists, **30–32**

C

calculations
  in bookmarks, **26–27**
  in form fields, 96
  in tables, **222–223**
callouts, 2, **61**
capitalization
  AutoCorrect for, 14
  dropped capitals for, **62–63**
  editing, **36–37**
  in form fields, 96
captions
  adding, **33–35**

for cross-references, 43–44
editing, **35–36**
in frames, 102
for links, 138
new features in, 2
for tables, 230
tables of figures from, **220**
case-sensitivity
in concordance files, 119
in file searches, 75
in sorting, 196
in text searches, 83
categories in tables of
authorities, **215–216**
cells in tables
deleting, 225
inserting, 225–226
merging and splitting, **226**
numbering, **229**
references to, 223
selecting, 230
centering
pages, **9**
text, 8
centimeters, 241
Change Case feature, 3, **36–37**
changing. *See* editing
chapters, cross-references for,
44. *See also* master
documents
characters
applying fonts to, **85–88**
for bullets, 31
position of, 87
spacing of, 87
special. *See* special characters
styles for, 206
Chart window, 38
charts. *See also* graphics
creating, **38**
editing, **38–39**

embedding, **39**
listing. *See* tables of figures
check boxes, xx
citations. *See* tables of
authorities
clearing
database search criteria, 47
file search criteria, 74
tab stops, 232
clicking, xviii
clip-art files, 107
Clipboard
for editing, **45**
for links, 138
closing documents, **52**
collapsing outlines, **169–172**
collating printing, 179
color
of borders, 28
of bullets, 31
of drawings, 61
of fonts, 87
of patterns, 29
of revision marks, 17–18,
186–187
of toolbar buttons, 238
columns
in indexes, 122
new features for, 3
newspaper, **39–41**
in tables
deleting, 225
inserting, 225–226
number of, 224
selecting, 230
width of, 224, **226–227**
command buttons, xx
commands, assigning, **160–162**
commas (,) in file searches,
77–78
comments. *See* annotations

comparing
database records, 47
document versions, **185**
concordance files, **119–120**
condensed character spacing, 87
context-sensitive help, **112–113**
continuation note separators, 93
converting
annotations, **11**
documents into master documents, 155–156
files, 4, **70–72**, 166, 168
notes, 91
OLE objects, **166–167**
tables, **223–224**
copying, 45
annotations, **11**
bookmarks, 25
with Drag and Drop, **58**
files, **80**
formats, **88**
help text, 113
link data, 137
notes, 92
styles, 17, **207–208**
toolbar buttons, 239
creation dates in file searches, 76
cropping graphics, 106–107
cross-references
creating, **42–44**
editing, **44**
in indexes, **123**
new features in, 3
for notes, 94
custom dictionaries, **199–200**
cutting, 45
bookmarks, 25
with Spike feature, 201

D

data files for Mail merge
designating, **148–149**
editing, **149–150**
databases
formatting, **48**
inserting, **46–47**, **49**
new features in, 3
queries for, **46–48**
Datasheet window, 38
dates
in file searches, 76
in form fields, 95
in headers and footers, 109
inserting, **49–50**
sorting by, 195
defaults
for display, **50–51**
for summary information, **211–212**
deleting
annotations, **11–12**
AutoCorrect entries, **15**
AutoText entries, **21**
bookmarks, **24–25**
caption labels, 35
cross-references, 44
drawings, 60
file search criteria, 74
files, 80
frames, 101–102
list items, 30
macros, **142**
mail-merge fields, 148
mail-merge records, 150
master documents, 156
notes, 93
page breaks, **173**
page numbers, **174–175**
search text criteria, 74

section breaks, 192
shortcut keys, **128–129**
Spelling dictionaries, 200
styles, **208–210**
table items, **225**
table of authorities citations,
216
in text searches, 84
toolbar buttons, 238–239
demoting outline headings,
170–171
descending sorts, 47, 195
descriptions
in dialog boxes, xx
of toolbar buttons, 238
dialog boxes
components in, xix–xx
new features in, 3
dictionaries for spelling,
197–198
custom, **199–200**
excluded words, **198–199**
directories
in file searches, 73–74
in opening documents, 168
in saving files, 202
displaying
annotation marks, **12**
annotations, **13**
bookmarks, **25**
defaults for, **50–51**
documents, **181–183**
field codes, **68**
file information, **76–77**
headers and footers, **109**
hidden text, **114**
mail-merge records, 150
new features in, 3
notes, **91–92**
Ruler, 182, 188
status bar, **203**

style names, **210**
summary information, 77
tables, **223**
dividing windows, 244
.DOC extension, 189
documents. *See also* files
closing, **52**
comparing, **185**
copying styles from, 207–208
creating, **245**
displaying, **181–183**
linking. *See* links; master
documents
mailing, **145–146**
master. *See* master documents
merging. *See* Mail Merge
feature
navigating, **52–54**, **103**
opening, **52**, **54**, 79, **167–168**
printing, 151, **178–179**,
181–182
protecting, 4, **55–57**
saving, **189–191**
selecting, 193
sorting text in, **195–196**
templates for, 54, **232–233**
windows for, **244–245**
Wizards for, **245**
.DOT extension, 233
double clicking, xviii
double spacing, 136
draft printing, 62, 180
Drag and Drop feature, **58**
dragging, xviii
Draw feature
callouts with, **61**
creating drawings with, **59–60**
creating text objects with, **60**
editing objects with, **61**
new features in, 4

selecting drawing objects in, **61–62**
drawings, printing, 180
drives
in file searches, 73
in opening documents, 168
in saving files, 202
drop-down lists, xix, 96
dropped capitals, 4, **62–63**

E

EditConversionOptions macro, 72
editing
annotation text, 13
annotations, **11**
AutoCorrect entries, **15–16**
AutoText entries, **21**
AutoText entry names, **21**
bookmarks, **25–26**
capitalization, **36–37**
captions, **35–36**
charts, **38–39**
Clipboard for, **45**
cross-references, **44**
display defaults, **50–51**
Draw objects, **61**
field codes, **68**
file formats, **166**
frames, **100–101**
graphics, **105–107**
headers and footers, **109**
index entries, **121**
links, **139–141**
list items, **30–31**
macros, **142–143**
mail-merge fields, **151**
mail-merge files, **149–150**
menu items, 161–162
newspaper columns, **40–41**

note separators, **93**
notes, **92–93**
OLE objects, **165**
previewed documents, **181–182**
protection from, **55–57**
repeating, **184–185**
shortcut keys, **128**
Spelling dictionaries, 200
styles, **208–209**
subdocuments, **157**
summary information, 80
table of authorities
categories, **215–216**
table of authorities citations, 214
tables of authorities, **216**
tables of contents, **219**
templates, **205, 233**
toolbar buttons, 239
toolbars, **237–238**
undoing, **239–240**
user information, **241**
effects for fonts, 87
embedding
charts, **39**
files, **165–166**
Ems, 241
endnotes. *See* notes
envelopes
addressing and printing, **64–65**
graphics for, **66**
in mail merges, 147
new features in, 4
equal-width columns, 40–41
equations for cross-references, 43
errors, spelling. *See* Spelling tool

even pages
  headers and footers for, **110**
  for section breaks, 192
.EXC extension, 198
exclamation points (!) in file
      searches, 78
excluded words dictionaries,
      198–199
exiting, **67**
expanded character spacing, 87
expanding outlines, **169–172**
explanations by grammar
      checker, 104
extending selections, 194

F

fast saves, 190
field codes, **67**
  displaying, **68**
  editing, **68**
  formatting, **68–69**
  inserting, **69**
  printing, 180
  updating, **69–70**
fields
  in databases, 48
  in forms, **95–97**
  locked, 70
  in Mail Merge, **148**, 151
  updating, 180
figures
  for cross-references, 43
  tables of. *See* tables of figures
FILEMAN.INI file, 81
files, **72–73**. *See also* documents
  concordance, **119–120**
  converting, 4, **70–72**, 166, 168
  copying, **80**
  deleting, 80

displaying information on,
      76–77
embedding, **165–166**
inserting, **124–125**
listing, 168
managing, 4, **79–80**
printing, 79
printing to, 179
searching for, **73–76**, 168
selecting, **80–81**
sorting, **80**
storing, startup preferences
      for, **202–203**
fill color of drawings, 61
filling in forms, **97–98**
filtering database records, 47
finding
  database records, **46–48**
  files, **73–76**, 168
  mail-merge records, 150
  section breaks, 192
  text, **77–79**, **81–84**
first page, headers and footers
      for, **109–110**
fonts
  applying, **85–88**
  for converted files, 71–72
  for dropped capitals, 62–63
  for envelopes, 65
  for heading numbers, 163
  for lists, 32
  new features in, 4
  for printing, 181
  shrinking, 182
  for special characters, 213
footers. *See* headers and footers
footnotes. *See* notes
foreground color, 29
form fields in protected
      documents, 57
form letters in mail merges, 147

Format Painter, 4
formats
 converting, 4, **70–72**, 166, 168
 copying, **88**
formatting. *See also* styles
 with AutoFormat, **16–20**
 captions, **36**
 charts, **38–39**
 databases, 48
 field codes, **68–69**
 frames, **100–101**
 heading numbers, 163
 index entries, 121–122
 with links, 138
 lists, 19, **30–32**
 page numbers, 174
 paragraphs, **177**
 sections, 192
 table of authorities citations,
  214
 tables, **221–222**, 225
 tables of authorities, 215
 tables of contents, 217
 in text searches, 84
forms
 creating, **94–97**
 filling in, **97–98**
 new features in, 5
 printing, 180
 protecting, **98–99**
 saving data for, 191
formulas
 in bookmarks, 27
 in tables, 222
frames, **99**
 adding, **100**
 editing and formatting,
  100–101
 for graphics, 107
 selecting, **102**
Full Screen view, 243

functions in tables, 222

G

global templates, 234
Go To dialog box, **103**
Grammar feature, **103–105**
graphics. *See also* charts
 in columns, 42
 converting OLE objects to,
  166–167
 editing, **105–107**
 for envelopes, **66**
 importing, **107**
 saving, **107–108**, 190–191
 selecting, 193–194
 watermarks for, **243–244**
greater than signs (>) in file
  searches, 79
gridlines in tables, 223
gutter margins, **23–24**, 153

H

handles on frames, 102
hanging indents with bullets,
  32
hard page breaks, **172–173**
headers and footers
 creating, **108–109**
 displaying, **109**
 editing, **109**
 for first page, **109–110**
 new features in, 5
 for odd and even pages, **110**
 for sections, **111**
headings
 for cross-references, 43
 numbering, 5, **163–164**, 171
 for outlines, **169–172**
 styles for, 19

for subdocuments, 156
in tables, **229**
tables of contents from,
   217–218
height
   of dropped capitals, 63
   of envelopes, 65
   of frames, 101
   of labels, 131
   of lines, 135–136
   of paper, 176
   of table rows, **228–229**
help, **112–113**
   for forms, 97
   new features in, 5
   for styles, 210
hidden fonts, 87
hidden text, **113–114**, 180
hiding
   annotation marks, **12**
   Ruler, 188
   screen elements, 182
   status bar, **203**
homophones in text searches,
   84
hyphenation, **115–116**
hyphens (-) in file searches, 78

I

icons with links, 138
illustrations. *See* tables of
   figures
importing
   chart data, 38
   graphics, **107**
inches, 240–241
indenting
   bullets, 32
   columns, 40

exact measurements for,
   117–118
in indexes, 122
and margins, 154
paragraphs, **117**
rows, 228
ruler for, **118**
indexes
   concordance files for, **119–120**
   creating entries for, **120–121**
   cross-references in, **123**
   editing entries for, **121**
   for help, 113
   inserting, **121–122**
   marking entries for, **119**
   page ranges in, **123**
   updating, **124**
Insert mode, **125–126**
inserting. *See also* adding
   automatic, **20–23**
   databases, **46–47**, **49**
   date and time, **49–50**
   field codes, **69**
   files, **124–125**
   indexes, **121–122**
   mail-merge fields, **151**
   subdocuments into master
      documents, **157–158**
   symbols, **212–213**
   table items, **225–226**
   Thesaurus suggestions, 236
inside margins, 153
Italic font, 85

J

justified text, 8–9

K

keeping text together, **126–127**

kerning, 88
keyboard, shortcut keys for, **127–129**
keywords
  entering, 211
  in file searches, 75

L

labels, **129**
  for captions, **33–36**
  for cross-references, 43–44
  in mail merges, 147
  new features in, 5
  printing, **130–132**
  in tables of figures, 220
languages for spell checking, **132–133**, 200
leading, **135–136**
length of form fields, 96
less than signs (<) in file searches, 78
levels
  in headings, 163–164
  in lists, **30–32**
  in tables of contents, 218
lines (graphics)
  for borders, 28
  between columns, 42
  in drawings, 61
lines (text)
  aligning, 9
  numbering, **133–135**
  selecting, 193
  spacing of, **135–136**
  as unit of measurement, 241
links, **124–125**. *See also* master documents
  creating, **137–139**
  editing, **139–141**
list boxes, xix

listing. *See also* displaying
  files, 168
  styles, 20
  toolbars, 239
lists
  bullets and numbers for, **30**
  editing items on, **30–31**
  formatting, 19, **30–32**
locked fields, 70
locking
  links, 141
  subdocuments, **158**
long documents. *See* master documents
lowered characters, 87

M

MACRO.DOT template, 142
macros
  deleting, **142**
  editing, **142–143**
  new features in, 5
  recording, **143–144**
  running, **144**
magnifying display, 182, **246**
mail, 5, **145–146**
Mail Merge feature
  designating data files for, **148–149**
  editing data files for, **149–150**
  editing fields for, **151**
  main documents for, **147–148**, **150**
  merging fields in, **151**
  new features in, 5
mailing labels
  in mail merges, 147
  printing, **130–132**
main documents for Mail Merge

creating, **147–148**
editing, **150**
merging data files with, **151**
manual hyphenation, **116**
manual page breaks, **172–173**
margins
  for dropped capitals, 63
  gutter, **23–24**, 153
  for headers and footers for,
    111
  for labels, 131
  precise settings for, **152–154**
  Ruler for, **154**
marking
  index entries, **119**
  revisions, **17–18**, 56, **186**
  table of authorities citations,
    214
  table of contents entries, 219
  table of figures entries, 221
Master Document view, 243
master documents, 5, **155**
  converting documents into,
    155–156
  creating, **156**
  deleting, 156
  editing subdocuments in, **157**
  inserting subdocuments into,
    157–158
  locking subdocuments in, **158**
  merging subdocuments in,
    158
  moving subdocuments in, **159**
  splitting subdocuments in,
    159–160
meanings of words, **236–237**
measurement units, **240–241**
menus, xviii–xix
  assigning items to, **160–162**
  shortcut, xviii, **162**

merging. *See also* Mail Merge
    feature
  revisions, **146**, **186–187**
  subdocuments, **158**
  table cells, **226**
mirror margins, 154
misspellings, checking for. *See*
    Spelling tool
modes on status bar, 204
mouse, xviii
moving
  bookmarks, **26**
  with Drag and Drop, **58**
  mail-merge fields, 148
  notes, 92
  outline headings, **171**
  subdocuments, **159**
  toolbar buttons, 239
moving through documents,
    52–54, **103**
MSFNTMAP.INI file, 72
MSSP2_EN.LEX file, 198
multiple pages, displaying, 182

N

names
  for AutoCorrect entries, 14
  for AutoText entries, **20–21**
  for bookmarks, 24
  for caption labels, 35
  for documents, 189
  for mail-merge fields, 148, 151
  for menu items, 161–162
  for styles, 208, **210**
  for subdocuments, **159**
  for table of authorities
    categories, 216
  for toolbars, 238
navigating, **52–54**, **103**

new documents, opening, **52**, **54**

new features, **2–6**

newspaper columns, **39**
adding, **40**
editing, **40–41**

nonbreaking hyphens, 116

NORMAL.DOT template, 210
AutoText entries in, 20–23
creating documents with, 232
saving, 190

Normal view, 242

NOT operators in file searches, 77

notes
adding, **89–91**
for cross-references, 43–44
displaying, **91–92**
editing, **92–93**

numbering
annotations, 13
captions, 34–36
cells, **229**
cross-references, 43
headings, 5, **163–164**, **171**
lines, **133–135**
notes, 89–91
pages. *See* page numbers

numbers
in bookmarks, 27
in form fields, 95
in lists, **30–32**
sorting by, 195

O

Object Linking and
Embedding (OLE)
creating objects with, **164–165**
editing objects with, **165**
embedding files with, **165–166**
file formats in, **166**
transforming objects with, **166–167**

objects
drawing, **59–62**
text, **60–61**

odd pages
headers and footers for, **110**
for section breaks, 192

offsets, binding, **23–24**

OLE. *See* Object Linking and
Embedding (OLE)

online documents, mailing, **145–146**

online help system, **112–113**

opening files, **52**, **54**, 79, **167–168**

option buttons, xx

optional hyphens, 116

OR operators
in databases, 47
in file searches, 77

ordering objects in drawings, 61

Organizer, 5, 234

orientation of paper, 176

orphan control, 127

Outline view, 242

outlines
creating, **169**
expanding and collapsing, **169–172**
moving headings in, **171**
numbering headings in, **171**

outside margins, 153

Overtype mode, **125–126**

P

page breaks
  adding, **172**
  automatic, **184**
  deleting, **173**
Page Layout view, 243
page numbers
  creating, **173–174**
  deleting, **174–175**
  in headers and footers, 109
  for index entries, 120, 122
  on status bar, 203
  for tables of contents, 217
  for tables of figures, 220
page ranges in indexes, **123**
page setup, **175–176**
pages
  centering, **9**
  keeping text together on, **126–127**
  repagination of, **184**
paper, size of, **175–176**
paragraphs
  aligning, **8**
  borders for, **27–29**
  creating, **177**
  formatting, **177**
  indenting, **117**
  line spacing in, **135–136**
  selecting, 193
  spacing between, **177–178**
  styles for, 206
  width of, 29
passwords for documents, **55–56**
Paste Link command, 137
Paste Special command
  for links, 137–138
  for OLE objects, 166
pasting, **45**

bookmarks, 25
  link data, 137–138
  OLE objects, 166
  Spike contents, **201–202**
patterns
  in drawings, 61
  in file searches, 75, **77–79**
  in text searches, 84
phrases, synonyms for, **236–237**
pica, 241
pitch for labels, 131
playing back voice
  annotations, **13**
points, 241
position
  of bullets, 32
  of captions, 33, 35
  of characters, 87
  of dropped capitals, 63
  of envelope text, 66
  of frames, 100–101
  of heading numbers, 164
  of menu items, 161–162
  of notes, 90
  of page numbers, 174
  of tab stops, 232
  of text boxes, 60
POSTNET bar codes, 130
predefined borders and
  shading, **29**
preferences, startup, **202–203**
preview samples, xx
previewing documents, **181–183**
Print Preview view, 243
printers
  for labels, 131
  setting up, **183**
printing
  annotations, **12**, 179–180
  AutoText entries, **22**

documents, **178–179**
envelopes, **64–65**
files, 79
help text, 113
hidden text, **114**
labels, **130–132**
merged documents, 151
previewing, **181–183**
styles, 179, 210
summary information, 81,
179–180
.PRN files, 179
promoting outline headings,
170–171
PROOF directory, 199
protecting documents
forms, **98–99**
new features in, 4
passwords for, **55–56**
text in, **56–57**

Q

queries for databases, **46–48**
question marks (?)
in file searches, 77–78
in spell checking, 201
quotation marks (")
AutoCorrect for, 14
AutoFormat for, 19
in file searches, 77

R

raised characters, 87
ranges, printing, 179
read-only documents, 55, 57,
79, 168
recently-opened files, listing,
168
recording macros, **143–144**

records
filtering, **46–48**
for Mail Merge, **150**
sorting, 47
redoing editing, **239–240**
removing. *See* deleting
renaming
styles, 208
subdocuments, **159**
repagination, **184**
repeating
actions, **184–185**
operations. *See* macros
table headings, **229**
replacing text, **15–16**, **82–84**
resetting
graphics, 107
shortcut keys, 129
toolbars, 238
return addresses
on envelopes, 64–65
on labels, 130
reverse printing order, 180
reviewing revisions, **187–188**
revising. *See* editing
revision marks, **185–186**
with AutoFormat, **17–18**
in protected documents, 56
reviewing, **187–188**
revisions. *See also* editing
comparing versions with, **185**
marking, **186**
merging, **146**, **186–187**
new features in, 6
protection from, **55–57**
reviewing, **187–188**
right-aligned text, 8
right-clicking, xviii
routing slips, 145
rows in tables, 221
deleting, 225

height of, **228–229**
inserting, 225–226
number of, 224
selecting, 230
Ruler, **188**
  for column changes, 40
  displaying, 182, 188
  for indenting, **118**
  for margins, **154**
  for tab stops, 231
rules in grammar checker, 105
running macros, **144**

S

saved dates in file searches, 76
saving
  AutoText entries, 20
  documents, **189–191**
  graphics, **107–108**, 190–191
  links, 141
  startup preferences for,
    202–203
scalable fonts for dropped
    capitals, 62
scaling graphics, 106–107
scrolling displayed documents,
    183
searching
  for database records, **46–48**
  for files, **73–76**, 168
  for mail-merge records, 150
  for section breaks, 192
  for text, **77–79**, **81–84**
sections
  adding, **191–192**
  cross-references in, 44
  for envelopes, 65
  headers and footers for, **111**
selecting, **193–194**
  Drag and Drop feature, **58**

drawing objects, **61–62**
files, **80–81**
frames, **102**
table items, **230**
sentences
  capitalization in, 37
  grammar checking, 104
  selecting, 193
separators
  for notes, **93**
  for page numbers, 174
  for tables, 224
shading
  applying, **27–29**
  for dropped capitals, 63
  for graphics, 106
  predefined, **29**
shortcut keys, xix, **127–128**
  deleting, **128–129**
  editing, **128**
  for special characters, 213
  for styles, 210
shortcut menus, xviii, **162**
Shrink to Fit button, 182
single spacing, 136
size
  of bullets, 31
  of envelopes, 65
  of fonts, 86
  of frames, **100–101**
  of graphics, 106
  of labels, 131–132
  of paper, **175–176**
  of table columns, **226–227**
  of text boxes, 60
  of toolbar buttons, 238
skipping
  grammar checker
    suggestions, 105
  Spelling tool suggestions,
    197, 200

slides. *See* tables of figures
Small Caps fonts, 87
smart quotes
  AutoCorrect for, 14
  AutoFormat for, 19
sorting, **195–196**
  files, **80**
  records, 47
sound annotations, 2, **10–11**, **13**
source documents for links,
      140–141
spacing
  of characters, 87
  of lines, **135–136**
  of newspaper columns, 41
  of paragraphs, **177–178**
  of table columns, 227
special characters
  with AutoFormat, 19
  for bullets, 31
  in file searches, **76–79**
  inserting, **212–213**
  in text searches, 84
spelling errors, AutoCorrect
      for, **14**
Spelling tool, **196**
  custom dictionaries for,
      199–200
  excluded words dictionaries
      for, **198–199**
  languages for, **132–133**, 200
  options for, **200–201**
  spell checking with, **197–198**
Spike feature, **201–202**
spin wheels, xix
splitting
  subdocuments, **159–160**
  table cells, **226**
  tables, **230**
  windows, 244
startup preferences, **202–203**

status bar
  hiding, **203**
  information on, **203–204**
  new features in, 5
strikethrough characters
  font for, 87
  for revisions, 18, 185
Style Gallery, 6, **204–205**
styles
  applying, **206–207**
  with AutoFormat, 18–19
  copying, 17, **207–208**
  creating, **208–209**
  deleting, **208–210**
  in drawings, 61
  editing, **208–209**
  for fonts, 86
  for headings, 19, 169
  for indexes, 122
  listing, 20
  for lists, 32
  names of, 208, **210**
  for page numbers, 174
  printing, 179, 210
  from Style Gallery, **204–205**
  for tables of authorities, 215
  for tables of figures, **220–221**
subdocuments, 155
  converting, 156
  inserting, into master
      documents, **157–158**
  locking, **158**
  merging, **158**
  moving, **159**
  renaming, **159**
  splitting, **159–160**
subjects
  entering, 211
  in file searches, 75
subscript fonts, 87
substituted fonts, 71–72

suggestions
  by grammar checker, 104–105
  by Spelling tool, 197–198, 200
  by Thesaurus, 236
summary information
  adding, **211**
  default, **211–212**
  displaying, 77
  editing, 80
  in file searches, 75
  for new documents, 190
  printing, 81, 179–180
superscript fonts, 87
suppressing
  line numbers, **134–135**
  revision marks, 18, 186–187
  Tip of the Day, 235
symbols
  with AutoFormat, 19
  for bullets, 31
  in file searches, **76–79**
  inserting, **212–213**
  in text searches, 84
synonyms, **236–237**

T

Tab key with tables, 231
tab leaders
  for indexes, 122
  for tab stops, 232
  for tables of authorities, 215
  for tables of contents, 218
  for tables of figures, 220
tab stops, **231–232**
Table Autoformat options, **48**
tables, **231**
  calculations in, **222–223**
  cell numbers in, **229**
  for charts, 38
  column width in, **226–227**
  converting, **223–224**
  creating, **224–225**
  for cross-references, 43
  deleting items in, **225**
  displaying, **223**
  formatting, **221–222**
  headings in, **229**
  inserting items in, **225–226**
  merging and splitting cells in,
    226
  row height in, **228–229**
  selecting items in, **230**
  sorting, 196
  splitting, **230**
tables of authorities
  categories in, **215–216**
  creating, **214–215**
  editing, **216**
  entries for, **213–214**
  new features in, 6
tables of contents
  editing, **219**
  from heading styles, **217–218**
  from other styles, **218**
tables of figures, **219**
  from captions, **220**
  new features in, 6
  from styles, **220–221**
TEMPLATE directory, 233, 235
templates
  copying styles from, 207–208
  creating, **233**
  creating documents with,
    232–233
  editing, **205**, 233
  for macros, 142
  managing, **234**
  for master documents, 155,
    157
  for opening documents, 54
  for styles, 210

text. *See also* fonts
  aligning, **8–9**
  for annotations, **10**, **13**
  from annotations, **11**
  in AutoCorrect entries, 15
  automatic, **20–23**
  for bookmarks, 25–26
  capitalizing, **36–37**
  for captions, 33
  for cross-references, 42–43
  for envelopes, 65–66
  formatting. *See* formatting
  for forms, 95–96
  in frames, 102
  in headers and footers, 109
  for help, 113
  hidden, **113–114**, 180
  for index entries, 121
  keeping together, **126–127**
  in lists, 31–32
  for notes, 90, 93
  for outlines, 169
  protecting, **56–57**
  replacing, **15–16**, **82–84**
  searching for, **77–79**, **81–84**
  selecting, 193–194
  sorting, **195–196**
  in subdocuments, 156
  and tables, **223–224**
text boxes, xix, 60
text objects
  callouts for, **61**
  creating, **60**
Thesaurus, **236–237**
tildes (~) in file searches, 77
time
  in headers and footers, 109
  inserting, **49–50**
  on status bar, 204
Tip of the Day, 6, **235**

titles
  capitalization in, 37
  entering, 211
  in file searches, 75
toggling capitalization, 37
toolbars
  creating and editing, **237–238**
  customizing, **238–239**
  mouse with, xviii
  new features in, 6
transforming OLE objects to
    graphics, **166–167**
typographical errors, checking
    for. *See* Spelling tool

U

underline characters for
    revisions, 18, 185
Underline font, 85, 87
undoing
  editing, **239–240**
  grammar checker changes,
    104
  new features in, 6
units of measurement, **240–241**
updating
  databases, 49
  field codes, **69–70**
  fields, 180
  indexes, **124**
  links, 140–141
  tables of authorities, 216
user information, **241–242**

V

vertical page centering, **9**
viewing. *See* displaying
views, changing, **242–243**
voice annotations, **10–11**, **13**

W

watermarks, 6, **243–244**
whole words in text searches, 84
widow/orphan control, 127
width
  of bordered paragraphs, 29
  of envelopes, 65
  of frames, 101
  of labels, 132
  of newspaper columns, 41
  of paper, 175–176
  of table columns, 224, **226–227**
wildcards
  in file searches, 73
  in spell checking, 201
windows, **244–245**

Wizards, 6, 225, **245**
.WMF files, 107, 138
word wrap in frames, 100
words
  hyphenating, **115–116**
  meanings of, **236–237**
  selecting, 193
  spell checking. *See* Spelling tool
wrapping in frames, 100
write reservation passwords, **55–56**

Z

zooming display, 182, **246**

Mail Merge Toolbar

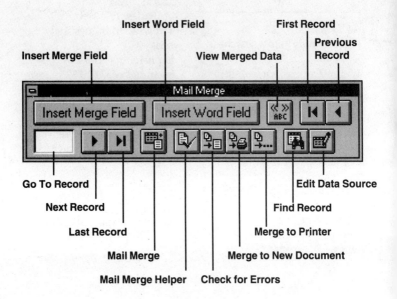

Insert Word Field

First Record

Previous Record

Insert Merge Field

View Merged Data

Insert Merge Field   Insert Word Field

Go To Record

Next Record

Last Record

Mail Merge

Mail Merge Helper

Check for Errors

Merge to New Document

Merge to Printer

Find Record

Edit Data Source

Macro Toolbar

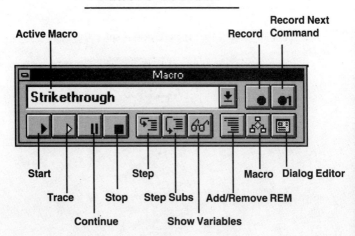

Active Macro

Record

Record Next Command

Strikethrough

Start

Trace

Continue

Stop

Step

Step Subs

Show Variables

Add/Remove REM

Macro

Dialog Editor